Historic Tales

of

MEDINA COUNTY

OHIO

Historic Tales

of

MEDINA COUNTY

OHIO

STEPHEN D. HAMBLEY, PhD

Foreword by Former President of the Ohio Senate Larry J. Obhof Jr.

THE
History
PRESS

Published by The History Press
Charleston, SC
www.historypress.com

First published 2022

Manufactured in the United States

ISBN 9781467151108

Library of Congress Control Number: 2021950605

Dedicated to my wife, Cheryl, and grandchildren, Jake, Lexi and Maddie. They represent my present loves and joys and my best hopes for a better tomorrow.

Photograph taken by the author.

CONTENTS

CONTENTS

CONTENTS

FOREWORD

When I moved to Medina County nearly twenty years ago, I fell in love with this part of Ohio. From its beautiful parks and lakes to its agricultural communities, to its bustling downtowns in Brunswick and Wadsworth and the historic Medina Square, this county had it all. I was happy to make Medina County my home, and although Ohio is full of special communities, I cannot think of anywhere else where I would rather raise my family. Medina County is also steeped in history, which you will soon discover as you read this book.

I have known the author, Stephen D. Hambley, almost as long as I have lived in Medina County. Steve is a longtime public servant who held office in both local government and the state legislature. We overlapped in the legislature (where I was twice elected to serve as state senator), and we worked together on many issues for our shared constituents. While I served as the leader of the Ohio Senate, Steve represented the people of Medina County (including me) in the Ohio House of Representatives. When I say that Steve is a "public servant," I mean that in the truest sense of those words. He has consistently put the people of Medina County ahead of his personal ambition, and he has served with honor and distinction.

Many who know Steve only through politics (as "Representative Hambley" or "Commissioner Hambley") may not be aware that he is also a historian and a former college professor. For roughly two decades, Dr. Hambley taught college courses on a range of subjects, including government, politics and United States history. He has carried that passion for knowledge throughout his time in office. He has also shared that knowledge with the public, often writing newsletter articles about the history of Medina County. Variations of those articles and other works make up the collection here: *Historic Tales of Medina County, Ohio.*

What a rich history it is. *Historic Tales of Medina County, Ohio* brings this history to life in an easy-to-read, accessible way. You will learn about Ohio's first tax deduction—a property tax offset that was earned by delivering squirrel hides to the township clerk, but it was paired with a penalty for anyone who failed to deliver the required number of hides. I discovered when reading a draft of this book that surveyors named the western part of Wadsworth the "Infernal Regions" because of its swampy and inhospitable nature perceived by early travelers. This, in turn, led to one of the area's streams being named "River Styx," which, over time, also became the namesake for one of Medina County's major roads and some of the businesses and parks along its path.

In *Historic Tales of Medina County, Ohio,* Dr. Hambley takes you through centuries of political intrigue that helped shape Medina County's communities, both literally and figuratively. This book shows the changing geography of the county over time and even some important (and interesting) near misses. You will read about a pre-Prohibition movement to annex Wadsworth into Summit County, which was motivated in part by the fact that Medina County had become "dry." You will learn about Cora M. Blakeslee, a politically active merchant who became one of the area's most prominent activists. Blakeslee's family-run hardware store, A. Munson & Son, used its advertising space in the local newspaper not to sell its products but to publicly advocate for women's suffrage.

This book tells the tale of how a Brunswick landowner preserved the area that is now Mapleside Farms—named "America's most beautiful farm" by a national travel publication—by pushing back against a public health nuisance. When a neighboring farm became a literal dumping ground, as the hogs there were being fed garbage shipped in from Cleveland, the landowner erected a billboard criticizing the situation and hired a man to protect his sign with a shotgun. The ensuing debate only lasted a brief time, but it had significant spillover effects. These effects included William G. Batchelder Jr. being propelled to a countywide elected office. Of course, Batchelder's son William G. Batchelder III shared his father's passion for politics and eventually rose to become speaker of the Ohio House of Representatives. One can only wonder how different Ohio's political history might have been but for this seemingly unrelated incident.

Historic Tales of Medina County, Ohio chronicles these events and many, many more. It is fun and accessible reading for anyone who wants to learn more about this great county, the strange quirks of state and local government or the important contributions made by social pioneers like Cora M. Blakeslee. Dr. Hambley has done an admirable job of bringing a diverse group of topics together into one collection. Enjoy your journey through Medina County's history with one of the county's longtime public servants.

Larry J. Obhof Jr.
president of the Ohio Senate, 2017–20

INTRODUCTION

The history of Medina County is full of long stories and short tales about people, places and events. For over two hundred years, many people who either ventured here or were born here have provided us all with examples of the good, the bad and the disagreeable of our human nature. The lessons we can learn from their stories are there for the taking, especially for those who honestly inquire, quietly listen and reflect on their relevance to our own experiences.

Many of the chapters in this book are extended versions of articles I wrote for *Helping Hands Newsletter*—a bimonthly publication of the Medina County Hands Foundation that is distributed to eleven thousand households free of charge. At the time of the publication of these articles, my major focus was to connect the history of our great county with the events and activities of the State of Ohio, largely with insight as a member of the Ohio General Assembly from 2015 to 2020. I have added additional stories and tales to provide a more complete picture of Medina County's past, and I have taken note of the role that some of our most prominent citizens have played in the history of Ohio.

I was frequently surprised to see heretofore unrecognized connections between prominent people and state events with Medina County communities and citizens. I always tried to find a relevance to those connections and, in effect, answer the interminable question of historical research: why is this important to know? My success in realizing that quest lies in the hands of the readers and future historians. I take responsibility for any errors of omission or commission in this work, but humbly ask for your forgiveness and understanding. I pray that such errors are few and far between, thereby relying more on a favorable review and appreciation of this work than the readers' tolerance for my own infirmities.

It is my sincere hope that the reader will share with me the belief that these stories of Medina County history continue to reflect on the continuity of our own cherished values—the importance of families, faith, education and democratic government. If we can agree to that, then my work has achieved much of what I sought out to accomplish.

—Stephen D. Hambley, May 16, 2021

Part I

CIVILIZING A COUNTRYSIDE

GEOLOGY OF MEDINA COUNTY

Vestiges of the Past That Shaped Our Future

*I*t can be said that the geology of Medina County not only defined our geography and the utilization of natural resources but also helped shape our history. It has likewise greatly influenced our lifestyles and our future. Nature defined where early settlers, who were reliant upon growing crops and living off the land, thrived. Rivers and streams, shaped over time with the combined erosion and deposition of soils and rocks by ancient glaciers, determined where pioneers best built their houses, barns and other structures, as well as plow their fields. Utilization of natural resources, like timber, clay, salt, aggregates, sandstone, followed by coal, oil and natural gas, would help shape the geography of the county, as well as enhance the economic vitality of its residents.

As noted Ohio geographer Alan G. Noble observed, the single most important factor in the development of the land surface of Ohio was continental glaciation. "Extensive sheets of ice covered Ohio during several widely spaced intervals of glaciation; the last one, the Wisconsinan, had the greatest effect on Ohio's present landscape."[1] Of the two divisions of Ohio, glaciated and non-glaciated, the surface of Medina County lies mainly within the glaciated plateau and unstratified glaciated deposits. The latter are commonly called till plains and are found in the northwestern part of the county (the present-day townships of Liverpool, York, Litchfield and Spencer).

Most of Ohio was covered in cycles by sheets of ice thousands of feet thick. The last cycle was called the Wisconsinan, which occurred between

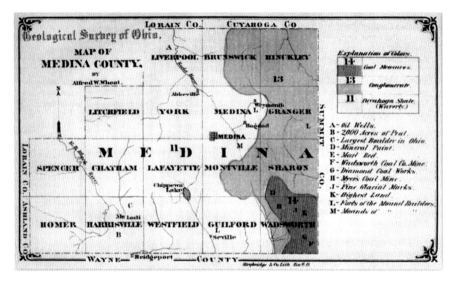

Map of Medina County from the Geological Survey of Ohio (1878).

fourteen thousand and twenty-four thousand years ago. The two main categories of glacial landforms—erosional and depositional landforms— occur either when the ice scours the preexisting landscape or substrate or when a glacial movement builds a new landform on top of the existing landscape by depositing sediment. Grinding away at underlying bedrock, the force of the advance and retreat of the ice moved the geologic materials. Sediments are left behind as the ice melts, which helps constitute the rich agricultural soils; deliver raw materials, such as clay, sand and gravel, for construction; and form extensive aquifers for groundwater. Erosion and weathering have reduced the constituent materials—ranging in size from boulders to silt and clay—and moved them accordingly across the landscape to help form valleys, hills, ridges and fields.[2]

In 1878, state geologist Alfred W. Wheat observed:

> *The economic geology of Medina County makes no great show. The mineral wealth of the county lies chiefly in coal. Of iron stone there is but little; and that contains only a small per cent of iron; and of lime there is a notable lack. Gas springs are known in nearly every township which is immediately underlain by the Cuyahoga shale, but it no case has this gas been utilized.*[3]

His observations about the commercial use of Medina County geologic assets were accurate for the time—coal was the chief resource. However, coal mines were limited to the southeastern portion of the county, and then they were only fully developed when the Atlantic & Great Western Railroad was built in the area in late 1860s. As historians explained the economic and population effects in 1881:

> *But the location of the Atlantic & Great Western Railroad, bringing these mines into connection with the great coal markets afforded by the cities and extensive manufactories of the state, not only made them sources of wealth, but, by developing an extensive business, added greatly to the growth and prosperity of the village, and of the township at large; a village by itself having grown up, composed of a population wholly connected with the mining and shipping of coal at Silver Creek, the point of shipment a mile and a half southeast of the depot.*[4]

The A&GW Railroad would be leased by Erie Railroad and would eventually operate under the New York, Pennsylvania and Ohio Railroad in 1880. Regardless of operations, the access of the coal fields to the greater Midwest and national markets enhanced its economic usefulness to the county and accounts for the growth in that area of the county for many decades. As subsequent chapters of this book document, the ethnic and political characteristics of the residents in the Wadsworth area would, at times, be decidedly different than those in central and western Medina County. Coal mining and factory worker families sometimes differed on key issues like temperance from those engaged primarily in farming and with more Protestant heritages.[5]

Coal mining in Ohio began around 1800, and during its first 150 years, it was an unregulated industry. Until World War I, coal mining in Ohio was conducted almost exclusively underground and largely by manual labor. These underground mining operations gained access to coal seams through vertical mine shafts that were up to two hundred feet deep, horizontal mine entries (drift entries) that were cut into hillsides at the coal elevation and through sloping tunnels that were angled downward from the ground surface. Early underground mines were small, discontinuous and poorly mapped.[6]

As depicted, Wadsworth and Sharon Townships had a number of these mines. According to Wheat, the mined coal typically reached a maximum thickness of nearly five feet. He reported that it was of superior quality and contained little sulfur. The production of just two of the principal mines in 1871 was over fifty thousand tons. Unfortunately, all of them were eventually abandoned and have since presented a considerable number of mine

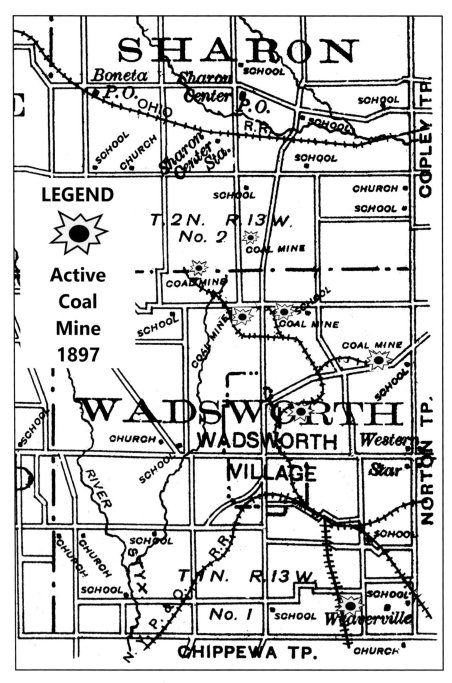

Coal production: Medina County ranked twelfth in coal tonnage in Ohio with 252,411 tons in 1886—up from 152,721 tons in 1885. At its peak, Medina County had nine mines employing 550 workers, largely based in Wadsworth and southern part of Sharon Township. *From the* 1897 Atlas and Directory of Medina County.

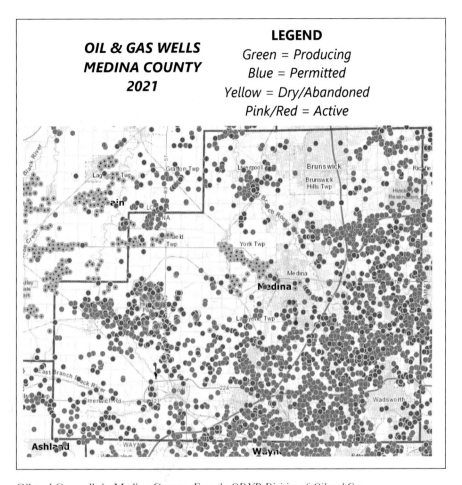

Oil and Gas wells in Medina County. *From the ODNR Division of Oil and Gas.*

subsidence issues for the generations that have followed—an unfortunate legacy of unregulated capitalism that is worth noting.[7]

In 1878, Wheat's comments about the relatively miniscule use of natural gas deposits would prove premature. The oil and gas exploitation craze in Medina County actually occurred in three primary booms: 1890 to 1918, 1920 to 1936 and 1936 to 1965. Each involved increased exploitation and well development efforts tied to changes in oil drilling technology and the economic cycles of demand with favorable market prices. For instance, the boom in the 1930s is partly attributed to the use of pressurized water to recover more oil than the previously used air pressuring techniques in the 1920s. Chatham, Harrisville and Litchfield Townships were most notable in those oil and gas booms, although active oil well-drilling and production has occurred in every township throughout Medina County.[8]

A big "oil rush" descended on the Chatham area in 1918, when hundreds of wells built by speculators on leased properties were precariously drilled. Reportedly, almost every lot in the township had an oil well with a pump. By 1920, thirty-five drilling rigs were operating in Chatham Township, but production continually decreased as the field played out until a new extraction technique called water flooding was used. The Chatham Field was one of the first to use water flooding after it was legalized in Ohio in March 1939. The figure on this page demonstrates the remarkable increase in production from the new technique. Many of the first projects occurred in the Berea Sandstone in the Chatham oilfield in Chatham, Harrisville and Litchfield Townships of Medina County, Ohio.

Unfortunately, while the newfound secondary extraction techniques that commenced after 1939 brought about a great surge of new oil from older drilled wells, the subsequent mismanagement of the wells and overuse of the technique led to widespread contamination of local water wells. Plagued by tainted and polluted wells, residents painfully managed the ill-considered legacy of this economic geology, for decades using ponds and cisterns for

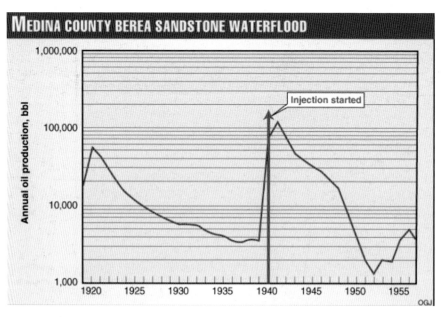

Success in Chatham led to the widespread use of the flooding technique and a surge in production. *From Thomas E. Tomastik, Search and Discovery Article no. 11341 (2020).*

A postcard picture of the largest boulder in Ohio, near Lodi. Medina PO, postmarked September 14, 1912. *Author's collection.*

drinking water. In 2003, the Medina County commissioners were able to expand public water services to the area after obtaining financial assistance from state and federal sources, as well as property owner fiscal commitments. The county added thirteen miles of water lines and an elevated water tower to meet the needs of these residents.[9]

One of the interesting features of Medina County geology that state geologist Alfred Wheat identified in his early survey map was the presence of one of Ohio's largest boulders in Harrisville Township, just northeast of Lodi. He identified it as syenite, a form of igneous rock, that was transported by glaciation from Canada.

> *This large mass of syenite shows two perpendicular sides; the highest of which measures twelve feet above the sod. One of these sides measures fifteen feet across the face, and the other is ten and a half feet across. The sloping side rests against a grassy bank, and gives access to the top of the mass. The depth of the boulder below the soil cannot be stated; apparently it is considerable, and perhaps the larger part of it is out of sight. If half of the mass is below ground, as can be fairly inferred, then the weight of the block can be stated at about one hundred and sixty-five tons.*[10]

Although a later newspaper report suggests that the boulder weighs closer to 195 tons, the more recently reported dimensions suggest that weathering is slowly reducing its overall size. An oddity, the boulder represents the great variety of geologic features in Medina County. It also provides a lesson to those of us who have likewise found ourselves here, much like the boulder. Possibly, it can teach us all that regardless of where you are from, when you plant yourself in Medina County, you, too, can be the biggest and best in the state of Ohio. Or maybe it's just a big old boulder that the last glaciers parked here until the next great geologic event, just waiting for nature to place it elsewhere on its next adventure across our globe. Unlike the eventual fate of the boulder, we have choices on how we weather our own storms.

OHIO STATEHOOD AND MEDINA COUNTY HISTORY

Facts We Think We Know

On March 1, 2023, Ohio will celebrate the 220th year of statehood, an anniversary certainly worth commemorating. The state of Ohio and Medina County have a celebrated history—one interspersed with stories that we know and stories we think we know. As a longtime history professor, I have often observed that what some see as "simple, indisputable facts" are actually a bit more complicated upon further inspection. History is rarely so simple and complete. I offer two examples to consider: Ohio Statehood Day and the current jurisdictional shape of Medina County.

Of all the important dates in Ohio history, March 1 is celebrated because, in 1803, the first general assembly met in Chillicothe to complete the official transfer of power from the federal Northwest Territory to the citizens of Ohio under its own constitution. It is a memorable date, for sure. However, according to some scholars, over the years, the Eighth U.S. Congress (1803–5) overlooked a critical part of the statehood process and failed to complete the congressional ratification of Ohio's first constitution in 1803.

In Governor Kasich's 2017 resolution recognizing Ohio Statehood Day, he mentioned President Dwight D. Eisenhower's signature on a congressional joint resolution of the Eighty-Third Congress, which confirmed the importance of this date. A resolution introduced by Ohio congressman George Bender on January 13, 1953, with hopes of ending all doubt, retroactively granted Ohio formal statehood back to March 1, 1803.

That's right—Congress retroactively granted Ohio statehood. As Congressman Bender explained in 1953, "The state constitutional convention presented the Constitution of Ohio to Congress on February 19, 1803, and Congress chose to ignore the whole business." Some might argue that Ohio was technically still part of the Northwest Territory until the passage of that resolution. However, for all practical purposes, it was the seventeenth state to enter the Union. While our state motto is, "With God, all things are possible," apparently, given this little tidbit of Ohio history, the federal motto probably ought to be, "With Congress, better late than never."

> FIVE CONCEIVABLE DATES
> FOR STATEHOOD DAY[11]
>
> April 30, 1802: Passage of Federal Enabling Act.
> November 29, 1802: Signing of the Ohio Constitution by convention delegates.
> February 19, 1803: Passage of the act extending federal laws to "State of Ohio" by the U.S. Congress.
> March 1, 1803: Organization of first Ohio General Assembly.
> March 3, 1803: Congressional resolution giving consent to the final modification of the Enabling Act.

COUNTY BORDERS: SIGNIFICANT BUT INVENTED LINES

As esteemed Ohio historian Dr. George Knepper observed in *Ohio and Its People* (1976), following the state's entry into the Union, "Ohioans were taking the first steps to organize state and local governments. It would prove to be an arduous and contentious process." As the state began to develop into a scattered array of settlements, it was divided into counties for the purposes of protecting property rights and persons. Townships and counties were formed for specific and often independent purposes. As historian and later member of the Ohio Senate and U.S. Congress Jay F. Laning explained in 1897:

> *Historically speaking, county government here came into existence before that of townships. Counties were organized for the purpose of establishing court districts, and county areas were defined about as soon as the work of governing the territory began. The first law for this domain was for the purpose of regulating the militia, and the second for organizing the courts. Those providing for the officers and affairs of townships came later.*

In their original creation and formation, county and township divisions were independent of each other, the townships not being required to first exist as a basic factor in forming the counties, nor the county to be, as it now appears, the aggregation of a number of pre-existing townships.[12]

After several organizations and reorganizations, Medina County was formed out of neighboring Portage County in 1812 and structured in 1818 with an area that would eventually be organized into thirty-two townships. Once formed in 1812, Medina County's earliest boundaries would remain in effect until 1822, while various townships would be settled and eventually organized into functioning local governmental units. As proprietors of the Western Reserve land offered tracts for sale at varying times and conditions, the county townships slowly took shape. Medina County did not obtain its current boundary lines until 1840.

Over the course of twenty-eight years, from 1812 to 1840, the general assembly altered county boundaries across the state thirty-five times. For Medina County, following its creation in 1812 and organization in 1818, it went through three configurations, as depicted in the following illustrations. Settlers came into Medina County at varying locations and organized into townships. With growth and development, new counties were formed out of pieces of township land formerly in Medina County—such as Lorain County in 1822 and Summit County in 1840.

Townships previously settled and organized in Medina County were detached and placed in Lorain County, Summit County and in Ashland County when it was formed in 1846. Interestingly, the current Medina County townships of Homer and Spencer were detached and placed into Lorain County from 1827 to 1840. When Medina County lost its entire eastern line of townships (Richfield, Bath, Copley and Norton) to the newly formed Summit County in 1840, it regained Homer and Spencer. Hereafter, for the last 180 years, Medina County has retained its shape with seventeen townships—although Brunswick Township was dissolved into the Village of Brunswick in 1960 and Brunswick Hills Township was formed by a massive series of detachments from the village in the same year.

The exceptional pattern of settlement within the Western Reserve was the result of how the Connecticut Land Company was organized and the distribution of the properties to the individual proprietors. Settlements were widely scattered, based on each proprietor's actions and resulting sales to families. Individual families, as well as groups of families, would venture deep into their assigned parcels in surveyed townships. Often, miles away

Medina County (2/17/1812 to 12/24/1822)

Camden Twp 1829 (1835)	Pittsfield Twp 1821 (1831)	Lagrange Twp 1825 (1827)	Grafton Twp 1816 (1818)	Liverpool Twp 1810 (1816)	Brunswick Twp 1815 (1818)	Hinckley Twp 1819 (1825)	Richfield Twp 1809 (1816)
Brighton Twp 1820 (1823)	Wellington Twp 1818 (1821)	Penfield Twp 1819 (1825)	Litchfield Twp 1830 (1831)	York Twp 1830 (1832)	Medina Twp 1814 (1818)	Granger Twp 1816 (1820)	Bath Twp 1810 (1818)
Rochester Twp 1831 (1835)	Huntington Twp 1818 (1822)	Spencer Twp 1823 (1832)	Chatham Twp 1818 (1833)	Lafayette Twp 1825 (1832)	Montville Twp 1819 (1820)	Sharon Twp 1816 (1831)	Copley Twp 1814 (1819)
Troy Twp 1835 (1846)	SullivanTwp 1817 (1819)	Homer Twp 1831 (1832)	Harrisville Twp 1811 (1817)	Westfield Twp 1817 (1820)	Guilford Twp 1817 (1819)	Wadsworth Twp 1814 (1818)	Norton Twp 1810 (1818)

Township Name
First Settlement Year (Organized Year)

Once formed in 1812, the earliest boundaries of Medina County would remain in effect until 1822. *Image created by the author.*

Medina County (12/26/1822 to 1/27/1827)

Lorain County

Cuyahoga County

				Eaton Twp	Columbia Twp	Strongsville Twp	Royalton Twp	Brecksville Twp
Camden Twp	Pittsfield Twp	Lagrange Twp	Grafton Twp	Liverpool Twp	Brunswick Twp	Hinckley Twp	Richfield Twp	
Brighton Twp	Wellington Twp	Penfield Twp	Litchfield Twp	York Twp	Medina Twp	Granger Twp	Bath Twp	
Rochester Twp	Huntington Twp	Spencer Twp	Chatham Twp	Lafayette Twp	Montville Twp	Sharon Twp	Copley Twp	
Troy Twp	SullivanTwp	Homer Twp	Harrisville Twp	Westfield Twp	Guilford Twp	Wadsworth Twp	Norton Twp	

Medina County 1822 to 1827. *Image created by the author.*

Medina County (1/28/1827 to 3/1/1840)

Lorain County			Eaton Twp	Columbia Twp	Strongsville Twp	Royalton Twp	Brecksville Twp
Cuyahoga County							
Camden Twp	Pittsfield Twp	Lagrange Twp	Grafton Twp	Liverpool Twp	Brunswick Twp	Hinckley Twp	Richfield Twp
Brighton Twp	Wellington Twp	Penfield Twp	Litchfield Twp	York Twp	Medina Twp	Granger Twp	Bath Twp
Rochester Twp	Huntington Twp	Spencer Twp	Chatham Twp	Lafayette Twp	Montville Twp	Sharon Twp	Copley Twp
Troy Twp	SullivanTwp	Homer Twp	Harrisville Twp	Westfield Twp	Guilford Twp	Wadsworth Twp	Norton Twp

Medina County 1827 to 1840. *Image created by the author.*

Medina County (3/2/1840 to Present)

Lorain County			Troy and Sullivan added to Ashland County 1846				
Cuyahoga County							
Summit County			Eaton Twp	Columbia Twp	Strongsville Twp	Royalton Twp	Brecksville Twp
Camden Twp	Pittsfield Twp	Lagrange Twp	Grafton Twp	Liverpool Twp	Brunswick Twp	Hinckley Twp	Richfield Twp
Brighton Twp	Wellington Twp	Penfield Twp	Litchfield Twp	York Twp	Medina Twp	Granger Twp	Bath Twp
Rochester Twp	Huntington Twp	Spencer Twp	Chatham Twp	Lafayette Twp	Montville Twp	Sharon Twp	Copley Twp
Troy Twp	SullivanTwp	Homer Twp	Harrisville Twp	Westfield Twp	Guilford Twp	Wadsworth Twp	Norton Twp

Medina County 1840 to present. *Image created by the author.*

from others, they would erect cabins, animal shelters and plant crops in preparation for winter. These were harsh and often lonely pioneer times. Occasionally, these families might be within sight of others similarly dedicated to founding these settlements within the wilderness. Towns were not formed going from east to west or north to south; rather, they were almost helter-skelter. This would be the pattern in Medina County, as well.[13]

As Ohio counties were being settled, a useful distinction in the historical development of local governments is to recognize that there were two forms—civil townships and land townships. As the *Ohio Gazetteer* explained in 1829:

> *But, when the state or county, in which any such lands are situated, becomes settled, the civil authorities of such state, or county, organize their townships, from time to time, for the purposes of civil government, in such form, and extent, as may best suit the convenience of the people. These are called, in this work, civil townships: while those, surveyed off by the general government, are called land townships. The limits of the civil townships often coincide with those of the surveyed land townships; but very often vary therefrom; sometimes including more than one land township, and sometimes less; according as the settlements progress, and the wants of the people require.*[14]

Once pioneers started to cluster in settlements within a land township, they could petition the county commissioners to form a civil township in which legal authority could be exercised to elect certain officers to operate the township. In the initial formation of legal townships, the general assembly directed the election of the following: three trustees, a clerk, a treasurer, one or more constables, a justice of the peace, two overseers of the poor, two fence viewers, two tax appraisers and a sufficient number of road supervisors.[15] Over the years, some of the locally elected offices would be eliminated and their duties incorporated within the scope of other township officials or county officials. These county officials would then provide those ministerial functions over the entire county and multiple townships, thereby providing for a more efficient government. Functions such as property assessment, tax collection, bridge building and maintenance, public assistance for the poor and indigent would eventually be taken over by the county government.

Medina County settlements, towns, corners, stations and neighborhoods took on names that residents would use for convenience and common reference. As was the custom of the Connecticut Western Reserve, such places were frequently referred to in contemporary accounts as towns and villages or stations, although they did not have the formal legal status of a village or township. Through the decades, as new people moved in, early settlers passed away, and memories faded; the names would likewise wane into obscurity. You can see some of these names preserved in present-day signage, like Bennetts Corners, Remsen Corners, Lester, Mallet Creek, Poe or Beebetown. Others, like Pliny, Coddingville, Paxton, Mongs Corners, Tanktown, Risley, Brants Corners or Dimocks Crossing, are just distant memories or small labels on fading maps—convenient and common reference points in the past, interesting facts to some but not historically consequential in the long run.

Statewide, townships as the rudimentary form of local government are celebrated annually on February 1. House Bill 652, enacted in 1998, designated the first day of February as Ohio Township Day to promote

UNDERSTANDING THE JIGSAW PUZZLE OF LANDS IN OHIO

Ohio is a jigsaw amalgamation of land grants from various sources largely bounded by the natural water barriers—the Ohio River and Lake Erie—to the north and south. There were twenty different land grants designated as follows: Congress Lands, United States Military, Western Reserve, Fire Lands, Ohio Company's Purchase, Donation Tract, Symmes' Purchase, Refugee Tract, French Tract, Dohrman's Grant, Zanes's Grant, Canal Lands, Turnpike Lands, Maumee Road Lands, School Lands, College Lands, Ministerial Lands, Moravian Lands, Salt Sections and Virginia Military Land.

A noticeable difference was the five-mile-square delineation for townships within the Connecticut Western Reserve versus the six-mile-square township layouts for many other parts of the state. Surveys in the Virginia Military Land were done using the metes and bounds method used in Virginia and the other original colonies, which often produced rather irregularly shaped parcels and jurisdictions. The only part of the state that shared the same size townships with the Western Reserve was the United States Military District that also used five-mile-square layouts. However, the rectangular survey system established by the Confederation Congress under the Land Ordinance of 1785 was used for most of the Old Northwest Territory. The Connecticut Western Reserve's smaller-sized units, however, were largely guided by the property owners and the Connecticut Land Company, not the federal government.[16]

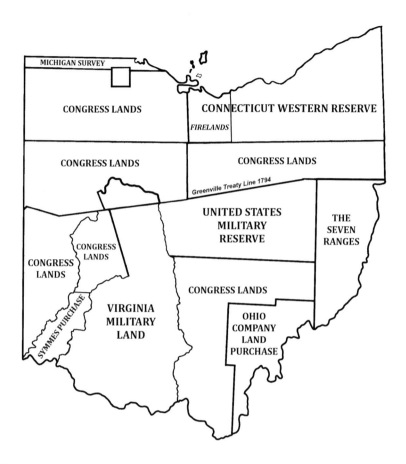

Major government-surveyed land divisions of Ohio. *Based on George K. Knepper,* The Official Ohio Lands Book *(Columbus: Ohio Auditor of State, 2002); "Map of Ohio Government Surveys,"* Atlas of Mercer County, Ohio *(Philadelphia: Griffing, Gordon & Co., 1888); E.O. Randall and D.J. Ryan, "Historical Divisions of Ohio,"* History of Ohio: the Rise and Progress of an American State *(New York, 1912); Ohio Division of Geological Survey, 2003 (2006), original land subdivisions of Ohio: Ohio Department of Natural Resources, Division of Geological Survey Map MG-2.*

grassroots governments and encourage organized efforts to educate adults and children on the attributes, as well as benefits, of townships. Starting as the foundational form of government in Ohio, our townships have evolved into efficient and effective providers of local services.

Modern township governments are under the direction of three elected trustees and an elected fiscal officer. They most commonly provide residents with services such as road maintenance, cemetery management, police and fire protection, emergency medical services, solid waste disposal and zoning.

According to the Ohio Township Association, Ohio townships in 2020 have direct responsibility for maintaining 41,000 miles of roads and streets and manage more than 2,400 cemeteries.

While each township in Medina County has a unique history, their respective timelines of events both stand alone and correlate with Ohio's own historical accounts. Some have suggested that townships were intended to be "temporary governments." There is no historical evidence confirming that statement from an authoritative source. In Medina County, the foundation of our current seventeen townships is historically strong. Residents and businesses alike located in these communities regularly take great pride and enjoyment in celebrating their respective histories, traditions and ways of life. Now that we have seen their origin and settlements that formed the outlines of Medina County, there is no doubt that any assertion that says they are merely temporary forms of governance is woefully unfounded—if not downright foolish.

3

EARLY CONNECTICUT WESTERN RESERVE

"No Man's Land" of National Politics

*P*rior to 1802, the Northwest Territorial legislature, governor and U.S. Congress were struggling over how and when the future State of Ohio would be allowed to enter the union. The two factions or parties, Democratic-Republicans and Federalists, were engaged in a political contest over the Ohio Territory, as well as the nation's capital. At stake was the eventual political control of the state and the balance of power in the U.S. Congress.

The underlying political struggle was quite visible between the Federalist territorial governor Arthur St. Clair as a remnant of his party's influence in the Northwest Territory and fights against a Democratic-Republican dominated Congress and White House.[17] Governor St. Clair claimed that the people of Ohio were "ill-qualified to form a constitution and government for themselves" and at the same time pushed a division act through the territorial legislature. Under this bill, if adopted by the U.S. Congress, Ohio would have been divided into two parts so that neither would have enough citizens to become a state and federal control could continue.[18] As mentioned earlier, the Eighth U.S. Congress failed to procedurally complete the congressional ratification of Ohio's first constitution in 1803. Prior to that, it also managed to defeat the division act and instead authorized a convention to create a new constitution for the state.

The precursor of this political struggle for Ohio's statehood was evident years before in the tale of the early Western Reserve, when it was officially not a part of the state of Ohio but rather a part of the state of Connecticut.

In a "phantom zone" of jurisdictional control that lasted for nearly five years, neither the State of Connecticut nor the federal government would assert control, protection or, most importantly for the owners of property, jointly acknowledge real estate property transfers.

For several major colonies, conflicts over land ownership extended back to the English sovereign grants of land westward from "sea to sea." Connecticut's charter, granted by Charles II in 1662, conflicted with Pennsylvania claims. Connecticut's claim stretched through the northern part of the Pennsylvania Colony, as well as the future states of Ohio, Indiana and Illinois.[19]

But Connecticut was not the only claimant to the lands west of the Alleghanies. In 1783, after the Treaty of Paris ended the Revolutionary War, the fledgling national government of federated states had to address the following claims of land:

- New Hampshire claimed the area of Vermont.
- New York and Massachusetts claimed western New York.
- Massachusetts included the "District of Maine" and claimed the southern portions of Wisconsin and Michigan.
- Connecticut claimed northern portions of Illinois, Indiana, Pennsylvania and Ohio (also known as the Western Reserve).
- Virginia included West Virginia, the "District of Kentucky" and claimed the central and southern portions of Illinois, Indiana and Ohio.
- North Carolina included the "Cumberland District," which is now Tennessee.
- South Carolina included a strip across northern Georgia, Alabama and Mississippi.
- Georgia included north and central Alabama, as well as Mississippi.

It took years for the conflicting claims, as well as agreements between the states necessary for the transfer of land property titles, to be worked out. The political battles between states over these conflicting titles seem petty and interminable in hindsight. For example, even after the Connecticut General Assembly finally ceded all claims in May 1786 to the Northwest Territory (except for the Western Reserve), it took Congress several months to accept it amid considerable opposition from New York and Virginia.

Although the northern portions of Illinois and Indiana ceded by Connecticut were accepted in 1786, it took Congress until July 1787 to organize the "Northwest Territory" from areas that would eventually become Wisconsin, Michigan, Illinois, Indiana, a majority of Ohio and northeast Minnesota. It was assumed that Connecticut, not the Northwest Territory, was empowered to exercise political jurisdiction over the Western Reserve. However, the lack of resolution was furthered by actions of the State of Connecticut and inactions of the national government.

On September 9,1795, Connecticut sold Western Reserve Land to the Connecticut Land Company for $1.2 million. One historian characterized the sale as a matter of desperation to unload Connecticut's "White Elephant."[20] The official report of a U.S. House of Representatives committee in 1800 stated: "And on the ninth day of September 1795, executed to the several purchasers, deeds quitting to them, and their heirs forever, all right title, and interest, juridical and territorial of the State of Connecticut, to lands belonging to said state, lying west of the west line of Pennsylvania, as claimed by said state."[21]

Oliver Phelps organized a group of investors as the Connecticut Land Company to secure the prize for the sum of $1.2 million with interest after two years from the date of contract. A deed of trust of the entire purchase was given to John Caldwell, Jonathan Brace and John Morgan. Under the agreement, future deeds from these trustees were the source of all land titles on the reserve.[22]

The congressional committee reported in 1800 that over the prior several years, there were many accomplishments: the claims by the Natives had successfully been extinguished, the land east of the Cuyahoga River was rapidly surveyed into five-mile-square townships and in short order, thirty-five settlements had commenced containing about one thousand inhabitants. Regardless, the problem according to the committee was that the earliest settlers under Connecticut's jurisdiction could not surrender their claims to the U.S. government as part of the Northwest Territory without endangering their titles. Despite questions about clear title, settlers still ventured into the reserve, creating even greater pressure to resolve the legal complexities. There was a movement among some of the investors to create an additional state out of the Western Reserve called "New Connecticut." However, once the State of Connecticut sold off the land, futile attempts to appeal to Congress left the pioneers in a legal no-man's land for years, as one historian described it.[23]

Even though the 1800 congressional committee had stated that the Native claims had been extinguished, it was never really that easy or unfettered. The company had dispatched Superintendent Moses Cleaveland with clear instructions and authority to handle potential disputes with the Natives. The company empowered Cleaveland with authority:

> *Over the agents and men, sent on to survey and make locations on said land, to make, and enter into friendly negotiations with the natives who are on said land, or contiguous thereto, and may have any pretended claim to the same, and secure such friendly intercourse amongst them as will establish peace, quiet, and safety to the survey and settlement of said lands, not ceded by the natives under the authority of the United States.*[24]

Historical accounts of the meeting between General Cleaveland and the Mohawk and Seneca Natives, headed by the famous Red Jacket and Joseph Brant, provide only partial assurance that the final terms reached by the parties for the territory east of the Cuyahoga River were fulfilled. While cash, cattle and whiskey were exchanged at the time, it remains unclear whether promises of either continual monetary support of the Natives by the federal government or a lump sum from the Connecticut Land Company were actually upheld. Regardless, the 1800 Congressional Report concluded the matter, at least to the satisfaction of the U.S. Congress. It was also satisfactory to Ohio descendants, as historian Upton boasted in 1910 that it was "a source of much satisfaction to the residents of the Western Reserve today that the title to the land was not stolen, but was bought and paid for, even if the price was low; further, that possession of the new country was given and taken under the best of feeling and without one drop of bloodshed."[25] Admittedly, that inevitable bloodshed and physical strife between the Natives and settlers occurred elsewhere in the state and the nation.

In the Quieting Act of 1800, Virginian congressman John Marshall was able to shepherd a deal through a treacherous Congress that was divided over the settlement. The division was primarily partisan and secondarily regional. In the House, 85 percent of the Federalists voted in its favor, while 83 percent of the Democratic-Republicans voted against it. Democratic-Republicans who voted in its favor—or against their party—were from the northern states of Pennsylvania and Massachusetts and the western state of Tennessee. Federalists who voted against their party and against the act were mainly from the states of New York, Maryland and North Carolina. In the end, it passed fifty-four to thirty-six in the House of Representatives.

Thirteen days later, the U.S. Senate took up the same issue, and the final tallies reflected the same partisan and regional tendencies—75 percent of the Jeffersonian Republicans opposed it, while 76 percent of the Federalists

All of current northeast Ohio became Trumbull County under the 1800 "Quieting Act," despite partisan politics and regional differences. *Base map (1803) from* Ohio House of Representatives, Membership Directory, 1803–1966 *(Columbus: State of Ohio, 1966), 19.*

favored the settlement. Both Republican senators from Tennessee voted against their party in favor of the bill, while Federalist senators from Delaware, New York, Massachusetts and Pennsylvania not only split with their party, but they also went against their fellow U.S. senators from the same states.[26]

As mentioned earlier, the underlying political struggle was quite visible between the Federalist territorial governor Arthur St. Clair, members of Congress and, after the general election of 1800, a new presidential administration under Thomas Jefferson. Presidential elections do not actually resolve the contest between political parties—they merely recast the characters into new roles in a never-ending struggle over power, property and status. Federalist governor St. Clair likewise struggled against a territorial constituency that was largely dominated by the other party, except for the southeastern part of the state and the newly adopted Western Reserve.

In the case of the Western Reserve, the Quieting Act of 1800, followed by the electoral demise of the Federalist Party, set the stage for the annexation of the territory of "New Connecticut," and it reinforced elements of the New England culture in previously settled parts of southeast Ohio. This "union of convenience" was naturally followed by the embrace of Democratic-

Republicans and more southern cultural influences in the forming of a state government with a typical Jeffersonian-Madisonian configuration and ideals. Structurally, it was comprised of a strong legislature, weak executive branch and judiciary dependent upon the general assembly.

This Jeffersonian-inspired structure would last at least until 1851, when a new constitution of reform was adopted, overcoming the intrinsic and human weaknesses the thirty-five "Ohio fathers" of statehood had molded. The early Western Reserve communities and culture remained important in the delicate balances of statewide politics and, later, the abolitionist movement, but in the end, it was the Quieting Act of 1800 that set the stage for the eventual amalgamation of northern- and southern-like cultures within Ohio.[27]

4

Squirrels, Property Taxes and the First Tax Deduction

Early in the history of our state, we had a lot of trees and squirrels. The forests of Ohio were so dense that it was often said a squirrel could climb a tree in Cincinnati on the banks of the Ohio River, jump from tree to tree and make it to the shores of Lake Erie without ever touching the ground. I'm not sure any squirrels actually tried to make that journey, but you get the picture. For pioneer farmers looking to cultivate as much land as possible as quickly as possible, once the trees were cleared, they faced a plague of these furry vermin that were very destructive to their growing crops. Historical accounts talk about the millions of gray squirrels that threatened the very survival of these fledgling farming communities.

Some might consider the enactment of the state's first property taxes as another threat to pioneers' early survival. In 1804, the Ohio General Assembly passed the first real property tax for the State of Ohio, dedicated for state government purposes. This was the original and probably only tax law enacted in the state of Ohio based on an assessment of the quality of the land. The land was divided into first, second and third characteristics and assessed uniformly according to the three qualities of value. As you can imagine, the system proved to be rather unsatisfactory for taxpayers, as well as legislators, and the general assembly tended to make amendments rather frequently. After all, creating the first means of taxation for the state would naturally encourage the creation of the first tax loophole to escape or reduce that tax liability.

In keeping with that legislative prerogative to tinker with tax law, members of the general assembly came upon a seemingly ingenious plan to help the farming communities and make the property tax laws seem less severe or maybe even more equitable. On December 24, 1807, the general assembly passed a law requiring every male person of military age to kill at least one hundred squirrels per year and deliver their hides to the township clerks when they paid their property taxes. If the taxpayer delivered the one hundred hides, he got a tax credit of three dollars—fifty dollars in today's money. However, anything less than one hundred hides meant that he would owe three cents per squirrel skin for not carrying out his civic duty in killing the fuzzy rodent. As an added tax incentive, additional hides beyond the minimum one hundred would be credited an equal 3 cents per skin on the next year's tax bill and could amount to another three dollars. The change in the tax law was a clever way to attack the squirrel problem, but it also proved to be a double-edged sword.

It seems that the "law of unintended consequences" legislators frequently talk about became very evident within a few tax collection seasons after the passage of this tax loophole. Apparently, it was a very easy thing for men to kill one hundred squirrels a year each. Likewise, almost every man in the state seemingly took advantage of lowering their property taxes in 1808 and

Ohio Statehouse pet squirrel postcard, dated 1916. Despite the brief bounty on squirrel skins, the statehouse grounds have become the ancestral home of many of these "urban pets." *Author's collection.*

the next year's tax bill. As one historian noted, "With the thousands of guns in use in the forests, the public treasury was in danger of being depleted, and the repeal of the law became necessary to restore enough ready cash in the treasury to pay the public expenses."[28]

The general assembly ended the tax break and eliminated the required squirrel hide bounty in early 1810. It did so probably not so much to spare the lives of our furry friends as to pay the bills of the State of Ohio. Most people recognize that taxes are a necessary evil. While, historically, tax breaks are a way for legislators to lessen that evil in the eyes of their constituents or friends, they are also often seen as a way to encourage specific behaviors. There is an old saying that if government doesn't like something, it taxes it. But on the other hand, if the government actually wants something to happen, it subsidizes it. Well, the next time you pay your property tax bill at the county treasurer's office, think of just how many squirrels benefit from a more enlightened approach to tax policy—one that doesn't link their hides to how much you owe. Some might say that it's just your hide that the government is after.

1816

Year Without Summer Helps Explain Early Growth of Medina County

*G*lobal climate change, *polar vortex*—phrases we hear frequently enough in the media now, but in 1816? Well maybe the words to explain killer frosts and extreme temperature variations have changed, but according to historical records, these climatological events accelerated the early growth of Medina County. At the time, many speculated that hostile climatic events came about due to the positions of the planets, the distance between Earth and the Moon, sunspots or maybe even, as New Hampshire governor William Plummer explained, the wrath of God. In hindsight, we know that it was the global impact of two successive massive volcanic explosions: those of the Mayon Volcano in 1814 and Mount Tambora in 1815—the largest eruption in the last 1,300 years. These two events, followed by a year of extreme temperatures, frosts, dry fog, failing crops and famine help explain why people from New England moved in greater numbers to the Connecticut Western Reserve in Ohio after 1816.[29]

Parts of New England reported the lowest recorded levels of surface and groundwater, as well as abundant wildfires. In the fall of 1816, Lake Champlain was reported at its lowest levels ever witnessed, local wells had generally dried up, wildfires raged uncontrollably in New York State from Albany to Ticonderoga and endless, sunless days were filled with choking smoke. In October that same year, Portland, Maine, reported to the world that in the counties of Oxford and Kennebec, from the Kennebec River to New Hampshire, fire scorched the woods, destroying everything and filling the skies with relentless smoke. One report stated that while ferrying

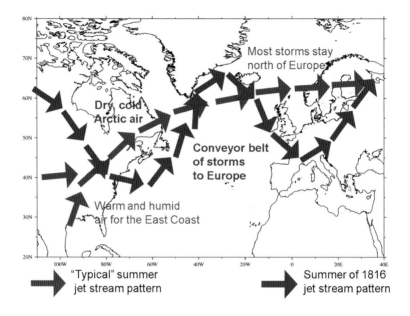

Jet stream changes from 1815 to 1816 that changed the climate of North American and western Europe. *Retrieved from www.northwestpassage2013.blogspot.com.*

across the Kennebec River, the smoke was so thick that the pilot had to use a compass to safely cross. Just as winter was approaching, the destruction of the forest led to a widespread shortage of wood for fuel.[30]

The average global temperatures decreased by about 0.7° to 1.3° Fahrenheit, and the Northern Hemisphere was the hardest hit. Identified by historians as "the last great subsistence crisis in the western world," hundreds of thousands of people starved worldwide because of repeated monthly crop-killer frosts and persistent "dry fogs." All of this was the result of millions of metric tons of volcanic ash, mixed with water and sulfuric acid, being ejected high into the Earth's atmosphere, obscuring the Sun and increasing the reflection of solar radiation away from the Earth.

The beautiful, rich and reasonably priced land of northeast Ohio was very attractive to the state's earliest pioneers. In contrast, the harsh and unpredictable weather conditions, exhausted soil and growing shortage of timber were significant factors that helped push the early settlers away from their New England homes. Temperatures dropped to as low as 40° Fahrenheit in July and August as far south as Virginia; meanwhile,

NOAH WEBSTER PREDICTS A DIRE BUT MANAGEABLE
WOOD SHORTAGE IN 1817

In a widely published treatise titled "Domestic Economy," famed
writer Noah Webster urged New Englanders to resist moving away
to the West, despite the "milk and honey" invitations and the
growing shortage of wood in New England. He stated in 1817,
"In truth, our country cannot sustain the present consumption
of wood for a century to come—we must either reduce the annual
consumption within the limits of annual growth, or the time will
arrive when we must search the bowels of the earth for fuel; and if
we are not able to find it in the interior of New England, we must
import it; or we must abandon the soil."

His treatise went on to urge the adoption of modern cooking
stoves, building homes of brick or stone rather than wood,
building chimney flues that are more efficient in the distribution
of heat within two-story structures and never burning green wood
because of its heating inefficiencies. Finally, he argued that New
England had more physical, civil, moral and religious advantages
than any other part of America—South or West. In the end, even
a shortage of wood and cold winters could be overcome by those
able to manage a "rigid economy" and be contented with "what
steady industry will furnish, and with those enjoyments which
reason and religion permit."[31]

communities throughout the northeastern United States reported extreme
temperatures ranging from 92° to 40° Fahrenheit in a span of a single day.
Drought followed killer frosts, wreaking havoc on people, livestock and crops.
Record drought conditions led to wildfires surging out of control and filling
the skies with smoke reportedly from New York to Maine. Tens of thousands
of people, hurt by the hostile climatic events, left New England states and
traveled westward into the Midwest in search of a more hospitable climate,
richer soil and better growing conditions.

Medina County did experience the so-called year without a summer in
1816, in which it snowed every month of the year. But New England and
elsewhere saw far worse. While Medina County people saw extremes and
unseasonably low temperatures, little else is mentioned in diaries and accounts
of the early settlers. Perhaps the harshness of pioneer life in the unsettled
country was already a given proposition for many of them. Regardless, early

NORTHEAST OHIO LANDS FOR SALE

- Cheap for prompt payment
- Advance Money on Connecticut Property
- Terms of payment made easy and agreeable

OHIO LANDS FOR SALE.

THE subscriber has for sale some very valuable tracts of Land in the Connecticut Western Reserve, State of Ohio, laying in the counties of Ashtabula, Geauga, Portage, Medina, Cayahoga and Huron—Also, 20 ten acre Lots in Cleveland. These lands are well worth the attention of purchasers. They will be sold cheap for prompt payment.   RICHARD W. HART.
Saybrook. 2 April.   6w76

LAND OFFICE.
THOMAS LLOYD,

PURCHASES and sells Lands in the Connecticut Reserve, state of Ohio, and offers to negotiate for the purchase and sale of real estate in this city and vicinity on commission, and will advance money on property conveyed with power to sell.
FOR SALE,
16,000 Acres of excellent Land, being in several different tracts and Towns in the Western-Reserve; terms of payment made easy and agreeable Also for sale, several valuable Houses, Stores and Building Lots in this City.
Hartford, September 16, 1817.   tf 47

Hartford Courant
(Hartford, Connecticut) Apr 14, 1818, Page 4

Northeast Ohio lands for sale, as advertised in Connecticut's *Hartford Courant. Image created by the author.*

growth in Medina County owed as much to climate change as it did to the availability of cheap, fertile lands ready for settlement.

Even now, people rarely move unless something is pushing them or attracting them. Imagine traveling hundreds of miles into a wilderness for a promise of a better life, fertile growing conditions and affordable land. As Noah Webster mentioned, invitations of "milk and honey" lives were promised, while simultaneously, pioneers were being pushed by harsh weather, failing crops and a worrisome economic future. The counties of the Western Reserve, like Medina, having been newly formed in 1812 and organized in 1818, were then ready to welcome these refugees of climate change with open arms.

The cultural pressures for westward growth should not be ignored, however. Other historians have noted that the same forces that governed the settlement of Connecticut also applied to the Western Reserve of Ohio. As Alfred Matthew observed in 1902:

> *The great westward pressure of Connecticut was in a measure resultant from the same forces that governed the settlement of Connecticut itself—that is, church secession and the desire for a more democratic government, both*

elements in the passion for freedom. But material conditions also entered into the complex cause of the exodus.[32]

Likewise, Matthew asserted that the combined demands for free education, town meeting democracy and the "federative" idea constituted Connecticut's contribution to the growing civilization within the Western Reserve, despite the physical hardships of weather and terrain. No doubt, climate change added to the motivations of those New Englanders who were moving to northern Ohio, but their cultural predilections similarly motivated them to venture out, shaped their new communities and kept them here.[33]

In the end, for the earliest pioneers, like Moses Deming of Liverpool Township, while it may have been the "deep snow, high waters, severe colds and mud" that compelled them to leave their homes, it was opportunity that brought them here and friendship and family that kept them in Medina County. As he reflected in 1847, "My life has been one of change; I have tested privations; I have experienced afflictions; I have toiled hard; yet when I think of the privations, the afflictions and hardships that others endured, I must frankly say, that a kind Providence has, in my old days, blessed me with competence, and surrounded me with many friends."[34]

Over two centuries, for the many people who ventured into Medina County and stayed, it remains a similar tale. Regardless of the various and changing reasons for being here, it appears that the attractions of family, friends and community keeps many of us here and heartens us to call Medina County home.

Part II

TRYING TIMES

TAXING BACHELORS IN AMERICA

More Than Money

*P*icking out bachelors for paying a special tax primarily because they are unmarried, if proposed today, would be met with swift criticism by many people in Medina County. I am pretty certain that a frequent comment on the suggestion would contend that this is unheard of and without historic precedent. Much to my own surprise after research, taxes directly placed on bachelors because they are bachelors have occurred globally and throughout written history, dating at least as far back as Greece and Rome.

The United States was born out of an anti-tax movement and historical skepticism for unequal and unfair taxes. The imposition of explicit bachelor taxes, as well as proposals to enact such fiscal penalties, occurred with surprisingly great frequency. Direct bachelor taxes in America began in colonial times and continued into the twentieth century. The author of one study found, however, that they declined significantly after the Civil War, although there was a dramatic number of proposed bachelor taxes submitted to state legislatures in the late nineteenth and early twentieth century. The study suggested that societal concerns about the institution of marriage and about the economic and moral health of society explains a flurry of such taxing schemes from 1895 through 1939.[35]

Sometimes, these legislative proposals were greeted with public derision and jests by incredulous newspaper editors and columnists. The *Medina Sentinel* included a proposal in Massachusetts to require bachelors to pay an annual tax of five dollars per head in a long list of "freak legislation."[36] The evidence is quite clear, however, that despite a very low success rate in implementing these tax bills in that period, their sponsors were serious. Their concerns and reasons often referenced biblical, moral, gender-biased and even racial rationale that reflected the impact of troubling times on their communities and families.

A typical example of this occurred in Wisconsin in 1909. A bill was introduced that proposed a tax of ten dollars a year after the age of thirty for all bachelors—this elicited a very credible proponent. The governor of the state strongly favored it for two reasons: "One is that the natural relation of adults is the married one, and that every normal man should obey the biblical injunction to make unto himself a wife. The other is that the bachelor does not bear his just share of the burden of taxation."[37]

In 1903, President Theodore Roosevelt evidently threw accelerant on the fire, so to speak. In a preface to a book about the poor working conditions for women, he suggested that "race suicide" was the most important question facing the country. He called on young men and women to become parents in order to prevent the decline of the country. The declining birthrate among Anglo-Saxons in America, as well as the rising tide of immigration, added to the social tensions of many people, despite Roosevelt never mentioning either in his treatise. The political reaction across the country made both points quite clear that it was a rallying cry on the campaign trail for the impending presidential election in 1904. The phrase attempted to counter some soft support for Roosevelt in several southern states because he was seen by many of them as too favorable to Black people. The anxiety created by his well-publicized "racial suicide" comment further fed those proponents of taxing any bachelors who were not doing their civic and patriotic part, as well.[38]

Some critics, in 1904, offered a number of reasons why the tax proposals were problematic. "The mere statement that there are 1,638,321 more men in the United States than women seems to be excuse enough for the bachelor; and yet, some of the states have already introduced legislative bills taxing or fining bachelors for their 'obstinacy,' and others are threatening similar action. Very well, then, the bachelors may say, if you will have us married, provide the brides."[39]

In 1921, the Montana legislature voted to tax bachelors three dollars per year. As the *Monmouth Daily Atlas* explained, "The taxers proceed on the assumption that all bachelors are a self-centered lot who have only their selfish selves to care for." The editorial continues arguing against the

Various Proposed Bachelor Tax Schemes in 1909

Missouri: A poll tax of ten dollars per year on all bachelors over twenty-five for the benefit for the state road fund.

Texas: Five dollars a year for bachelors over twenty-five and under thirty; ten dollars for all over thirty-five and under forty. All over forty to be exempt.

Massachusetts: From twenty to twenty-five years, five dollars a year; from twenty-five to thirty, ten dollars; thirty to thirty-five, fifteen dollars; thirty-five to forty, twenty dollars; over forty, chloroforming.

Wisconsin: Ten dollars a year after the age of thirty.

Iowa: After forty, twenty-five dollars a year; after forty-five, thirty dollars; after fifty-five, exempt.

Indiana: From twenty-five to thirty, $2.50 a year; thirty to thirty-five, $4.00; thirty-five to forty, $5.00; forty to sixty, $7.00.

Illinois: Five dollars a year for all over thirty.

Source: *Baltimore Sun*. "Legislatures of Many States Are Considering Bills Planned to Tax the Carefree Bachelor Out of Existence." March 7, 1909, 13.

proposal, suggesting, "And what of those bachelors who think they serve society in that by making no choice of a wife they avoid making a bad choice. Such a policy deserves, at least, respect and consideration."[40]

You may ask, "What about Ohio?" According to esteemed historian J.H. Galbreath, Ohio as a territory had a bachelor tax for a couple of years. Essentially, when it was enacted on December 8, 1800, it served as a poll tax. However, it was so unpopular that when the Ohio Constitutional Convention met in 1802, a provision was inserted that prohibited it. The original territorial poll tax was a bit complicated, but it was one that penalized the bachelor. Every able-bodied male over twenty-one years of age owed a poll tax of $0.50 annually, married or unmarried. In addition, unmarried able-bodied men over twenty-one years of age owed another $2.50 per year, unless they had a property wealth worth $200.00 or more and paid taxes on that property. Essentially, if you were a bachelor without taxable, real property, you owed the state the additional money for the privilege of citizenship, voting rights and, of course, being single.[41]

Given the strength and consistency of the constitutional provisions against poll taxes in Ohio, the state largely resisted the seemingly relentless proposals to use taxes against a class of men who chose not to marry. It doesn't mean that preferential tax treatment of married and child-producing couples wasn't sought or implemented, of course. Regardless, amid the national wave of bachelor taxing proposals, there was a brief attempt to include such a provision in the Ohio Constitution during the proceedings of the 1912 convention. Democrat Stanley E. Bowdle, a lawyer from Cincinnati, made a rather convoluted attempt to get around the poll tax prohibition and instead treat bachelorhood as a valuable franchise in order to tax it. His speech at the convention was quite enlightening:

By a conspiracy among the bachelors in this convention, my bachelor tax proposal was tabled Saturday when I was absent from this convention. I submitted that proposition in the most serious spirit. It deserved consideration. Ohio has ten thousand bachelors above thirty years of age who persist in their bachelorhood in spite of the feminine beauty which assails them on every side. The loss to the commonwealth through their persistency is simply incalculable. This convention does not seem to have discovered the subtle purpose of my proposal. I had planned by this deft move to add greatly to the population and happiness of the state by driving men into a state productive of both.

We have in Ohio a poll tax inhibition. Now, attacks on bachelors may be described as a poll tax. I had determined in my proposal to treat bachelorhood as valuable franchise and tax it as such. After thirty-five years, men become cold, calculating, and selfish. I want to help them to become warm, thoughtful, and un-selfish. For certainly, marriage is the result of that delightful thoughtfulness which providence has arranged to relieve life of its tragic somberness. I, therefore, move you that the vote by which this proposal was tabled be reconsidered.[42]

The motion was lost.

In a brief newspaper account of the proposal, Bowdle further elaborated his thoughts that if the tax was adopted, "women would be economically provided for and that the most potent reason for women suffrage would have been met. His proposal would have taxed bachelors and bachelorhood and the evils arising therefrom."[43] Obviously, his proposal, if not his rationale, found effectively little support with one possible exception. Frank W. Woods, a convention delegate from Medina, tried to have the tax proposal referred

Images depicting bachelors in rather unflattering ways, as seen below, which shows them as overweight men drinking a lot of beer, aided by mechanical means to consume great quantities through a "beer lift," were prevalent and indicative of a widespread prejudice. Of course, they deserved to be taxed more for their less-than-virtuous lifestyle, a temperance-minded married person might argue. Herbert's Bachelor Hotel in San Francisco, established in 1909, did not allow women to stay in the hotel or visit the dining room—except on one occasion to help a local charity raise money. It exclusively served men until 1933. It was renowned for its accommodations that kept with male tastes and fraternity. Drinking beer in great quantities was apparently portrayed as a typical example of both.[45]

A postcard promoting Herbert's Bachelor Hotel in San Francisco. It depicts bachelors in a stereotypical and unflattering way. *Author's collection.*

to a special committee chaired by Henry Eby, a farmer and bachelor from Preble County, instead of being tabled. His motion and attempt to keep it open for discussion, however, did not prevail.[44]

Following his service in the convention, Bowdle benefited from the 1912 split of the Republican Party and was elected to one term as U.S. congressman. His brief term of office demonstrated that he had no fear in proposing tax policies for purposes of penalizing the wealthy and promoting societal norms. In 1914, he sponsored legislation that would impose a high-income tax—25 percent on all incomes from property within the United States—on any woman who wedded a foreign noble with a title, a so dubbed "titled heiress." According to newspaper accounts, he had purposely intended to harass the fathers of women from several prominent wealthy American families who had married off their daughters to European royalty. He contended that they didn't marry for love but for societal and monetary advancement. Apparently, he was offended when "the lure of royalty draws the wealthy daughters of America" and was willing to use federal tax policy to rebuke that trend. In 1914, he was defeated for reelection by his former Republican opponent. Although he later moved into an adjoining congressional district, as a staunch supporter of progressive President Woodrow Wilson, he again lost in 1916 to another Republican candidate, Captain Victor Heintz.[46]

Aside from the moral arguments and proposed benefits of married men, the public purpose for a bachelors' tax had a wide range of uses—not necessarily forcing bachelors to marry. Payment for support of various "needy" in congregate settings or homes, like unwed mothers, unmarried women, orphaned children and widows was common. It was a means of providing funding within the states for institutions that have now become antiquated and whose purposes are outdated notions, but they are still recognizable as needing societal assistance. Our current "social safety net" of cash resources and programs for women with children, the unemployed or underemployed single woman and parentless children remain recognizable descendants of those state initiatives. The one item that doesn't remain, thankfully, is the concept of penalizing men because they are single.

As Kornhauser found in her 2012 study, the primary motivation for the special tax on bachelors was never just about the revenue. The main justification, as she stated, was that "bachelors deserved to be taxed because they were failing their moral, social, and civic duty to settle down, marry and produce future citizens." Rather than bachelor taxes, society and the American system of taxation policy since the 1930s has shifted in favor of tax bonuses to promote marriage and children—the carrot, rather than the stick approach.[47]

The lesson is that, despite our protestations and philosophic preferences, tax laws in our republic are frequently subjective and changing. Tax loopholes are easy prey for elected representatives who are answerable to a public with attitudes, prejudices and goals who seek to keep their own tax liabilities to the minimum while making someone else pay "their fair share" for the government services we all demand and expect. One might suggest that that is the history of our great country, which seems to have remained fairly consistent, despite our efforts to continuously redefine which group deserves that adverse tax treatment.

He Was Many Things, but Not a Jolly Giant

Captain Martin Van Buren Bates

*A*s many know, nineteenth-century Medina County became home to world-famous giants Captain Martin Van Buren Bates and Anna Hannon Swan Bates. In their primes, Martin claimed to be seven feet, eleven and a half inches tall and tipped the scales at 478 pounds, while Anna daintily measured the same height and around 430 pounds. Varying newspapers claimed that Anna was an inch taller than Martin on the day of their wedding and that Martin was a reported mere seven feet, eight inches tall. Promotional considerations typically used by the nineteenth-century entertainment industry aside, at the time of his death in 1919, at the age of seventy-four, Martin measured seven feet, four inches tall and weighed 380 pounds after spending several months ill and bedridden. By every measure, Martin and Anna were giants among all people.

According to Guinness Records' authoritative declaration as the "world's tallest couple," they retain their world fame even a century later. There are many stories behind their individual origins, show business careers with P.T. Barnum and W.W. Cole's Circus and chosen farmer's life in Guilford Township and nearby Seville Village. Together, they toured the world, entertained and dined with English, Russian and other European royalty while performing before hundreds and thousands of people. Anna was a proficient pianist, excelled at acting and was an expert lecturer on giants and literature. In their attempt to settle down, a farmhouse in Guilford Township was built and furnished in 1873 to equal their stature—twelve-foot-high ceilings on the first and second floors, eight-foot-six-inch-high doorways,

Left: Captain Martin Van Buren Bates, his second wife, Annette, and Frank Bowman in 1908. (Bowman was around four feet tall.) *Courtesy of Medina County Historical Society.*

Right: Giantess Anna Swan Bates. *Courtesy of Medina County Historical Society.*

a ten-foot-long bed and chairs that could fit three adults. They had a proportionately large carriage built that was drawn by six stout Norman or Clydesdale horses.[48]

Their wedding in England not only received international newspaper coverage, but their marriage benefited from royal patronage and objects of personal affection. They were married at the Parish of St. Martin-in-the-Fields, Trafalgar Square, London, England, on June 17, 1871, in an exclusive, well-attended but brief ceremony. Queen Victoria gifted Martin the "Kentucky Giant," a massive gold watch made by E.W. Streeter of London that had hourly chimes and was valued, at the time, around £500. The case weighed nine ounces, the watch weighed over a pound and, with the neck chain, it weighed over three pounds. Anna, the "Nova Scotia Giantess" received a cluster diamond ring with several large jewels from England's much-loved queen. The ring was also likely procured from E.W. Streeter, as he was a highly regarded diamond, goldsmith and jewelry retailer favored by upper-crust society in London at that time. As you can imagine, Martin and Anna treasured these unique gifts for their entire lives. After his death in

1919, Bates's second wife sold his watch and the diamond ring to a Medina jeweler, and the bridal gifts have since disappeared from public view.[49]

Show business was good for the couple, as it allowed them to perform as individuals. But the giant and giantess showbiz reputations often softened the more harsh and severe reputation Captain Bates had earned during and after the Civil War. Both Anna and Martin were active in the local Baptist church. They preferred their attendance and Christian acts to not draw unnecessary public attention. Anna was baptized in the church baptistry with little public ceremony and taught Sunday Bible school. They also had a special pew in the third row that had been remodeled to accommodate their large size, so they did not have to "stand out" during services. Being renowned giants and trying to live with a semblance of privacy did present some challenges.

Of the two, Martin Van Buren ferociously earned a reputation and eventual rank as a Confederate captain. While he was growing in stature starting in his teens, he peaked around the age of twenty-seven. His fearful temper and profoundly violent actions in wartime and during the vicious era of the Civil War in Kentucky provided an insight to the man that is not frequently mentioned in Medina County history.

Kentucky communities were deeply divided during the Civil War, and intrastate violence was commonplace. At first, Kentucky declared official neutrality, but by late 1861, the Confederacy had established long defensive lines across the state. The Confederacy repeatedly attempted to take control of the state, but eventually, Kentucky declared itself loyal to the Union cause. The state government was divided, as were the state's citizens. Violence on behalf of either side was common. However, vengeance for transgressions against family members was routine, expected and increasingly brutal. Violence bred violence, plain and simple. Avid Unionists and Confederates were abundant throughout Kentucky—many times, in the same communities, churches or even families—and successive violence between the two sides was sadly commonplace.

Martin Van Buren Bates, for a brief time before the Civil War, taught in a small log schoolhouse near the Bateses' family farm in Kona, Letcher County, Kentucky. As the story goes, he was the eleventh and youngest child and did not demonstrate any growth spurt until seven years of age. He grew so fast—first fat and then tall—that his parents feared for his health and spared him the farming chores the other children were required to perform. Martin instead concentrated on his education and recitation skills and developed a reputation for having a photographic memory. He was educated at Emma-Henry College in Washington County, Virginia. By his early twenties, he

BIGGEST SHIRT IN
AMERICA?

A Catskill shirt company claimed it had made the largest garment of its kind in America for Captain Martin Van Buren Bates. Its dimensions were as follows: length, 74.00 inches; waist, 66.50 inches; neck, 26.00 inches; wristband, 18.00 inches; sleeves from middle of back, 63.00 inches. It took nearly 6.00 yards of muslin and 1.75 yards wide.

Source: *Cleveland Plain Dealer*. "News." May 22, 1882, 6.

had passed the exams required for a teaching certificate and used his mental and physical prowess to educate and impress discipline on the students. "Big Boy Bates," as he was called then, reportedly didn't get any sass from the young students, and his bellowing voice undoubtedly demanded attention.

As Bates explained in his autobiography, published in 1880, "The son of a slave owner, with the principle of states' rights predominating within me, I felt it my duty to tender my services in defense of what I believed the right." It was not an uncommonly expressed explanation for former Confederate soldiers, nor rare for a Kentucky-born-and-raised citizen. Although, after the war, in August 1865, it was reported in the *Louisville Journal* that Bates would genuinely fight on the side of the federal government against the world if he should be called on to do so. Political prisoners and Confederate prisoners of war were often released after taking an "oath of allegiance." Such public pronouncements were expected in northern society shortly after the war, as were conditions for the eventual reinstatement of voting rights in former Confederate states.[50]

In September 1861, Bates joined the Confederate army as a private in the Fifth Kentucky Infantry for a year. A series of battlefield promotions to the rank of first lieutenant followed his demonstrated fierceness in battles all over the state. It was said that "that Confederate giant who's as big as five men and fights like fifty" had a truly terrifying appearance—and reputation. Supposedly, he wielded two large .71-caliber horse pistols strapped across his chest. They were made specifically for him at the Tredegar Iron Works in Richmond. He also sported an extra-long saber that measured eighteen inches beyond the standard size. His horse was a Percheron that had been "acquisitioned" from a German farmer in Pennsylvania. Originally bred for warfare, these draft horses are well-muscled and known for their intelligence and willingness to work. It was certainly a fitting ride for the "Kentucky Giant," as he was increasingly being called—"Big Boy Bates" didn't quite conjure the same respect on the battlefield.

A map of Camp Chase near Columbus, Ohio, by A. Ruger, Company H, 88 Reg. OVI. Copy of a lithographic print by Ehrgott, Forbriger & Co. of Cincinnati, Ohio. *Author's collection.*

In April 1863, Bates was wounded and captured by Union forces in Piketon, Kentucky. He was moved to Camp Chase in Columbus, Ohio, in April and then to City Point, Virginia, where he was exchanged for captured Union soldiers on May 13. From July 1862 to July 30, 1863, captured Confederate and Union soldiers were frequently and regularly exchanged to conciliate the issues and costs of guarding and quartering prisoners and to minimize the logistical difficulty of moving prisoners.

Some subsequent newspaper accounts contend that the "Kentucky Giant" escaped and then joined Company A of the Seventh Confederate Calvary. He entered with the rank of first lieutenant along with his brother Captain Robert Bates under Lieutenant Colonel Clarence Prentice. The record is clear that he did indeed join up with the Seventh Confederate Calvary after his captivity—but so did several other captives from his former Kentucky unit, as they met Colonel Prentice during their brief stay at Camp Chase in Ohio. However, the Civil War military records clearly provide sufficient evidence of a prisoner exchange, rather than an escape.[51]

TREATMENT OF POW "KENTUCKY GIANT" CAPTAIN BATES MAY HAVE NOT BEEN SO BAD

While "Kentucky Giant" Lieutenant Martin Van Buren Bates was briefly held as a prisoner of war at Camp Chase, near Columbus, Ohio, as an officer, he was entitled to preferential treatment. According to reports, Confederate officers at Camp Chase were permitted to wander throughout the Columbus area, register at local hotels, receive gifts of food and money and even visit sessions of the Ohio Senate, provided they submitted to an "oath of honor." There were over eight thousand prisoners confined at Camp Chase at its highpoint in 1863, while hundreds of those incarcerated in the beginning included political prisoners.[52]

The most memorable Civil War tale of Bates's ferocity occurred when Martin returned to the family farm near Whitesburg, Kentucky, while on leave in 1864. Local Unionist sympathizers had kidnapped one of his brothers and tortured him to death with their bayonets. Martin gathered up his comrades, and together, they rounded up the eight supposed killers, along with their wives, children, parents and grandparents. They marched them to a spot called Big Hollow, held them overnight and constructed a crude but massive "gallows" to hang the eight culprits. The gallows consisted of a horizontal pole that was strapped about ten feet above the ground between two slim oak trees that had grown twelve feet apart.

Despite cries and pleas for mercy, Martin mounted his giant horse and had his men herd the bound prisoners to a beech log on the ground directly beneath the crude gallows. After placing the eight nooses around the killers' necks, Bates raised his hand in a signal, and thereupon, two men shoved the log, causing it to roll down the hill. The eight men dropped a few inches and slowly choked to death while onlooking family members were held back from rescuing their loved ones with swords and cocked pistols.

According to eyewitnesses, the Kentucky Giant warned the grieving families that the rotting bodies were to remain untouched at these gallows as a brutal reminder of the price of killing a Bates. He also stated that anyone who violated his order would not only suffer the same fate, but their family would also be destroyed, their homes burned and stock killed. It was only when Martin returned after the war in 1865 that he verified the boney remains were still hanging. Having confirmed that his directives were followed, he was persuaded to allow the families to finally bury the executed victims.

Stating that he wanted no part of the local feuds and bloodshed within the surrounding area of his homeland, Martin wisely left Kentucky for good and traveled to Cincinnati, where he began working in Robinson's Circus. There is no doubt that he was mindful that the families of the lynched men would eventually seek revenge for his brutal acts, regardless of his physical stature. He told his nephew John Wright at the time, "I've seen enough bloodshed. I don't want any more." After all, even the stories of mythical and biblical giants demonstrate repeatedly that they are also mortal.[53]

Bates never mentioned these horrific events in his autobiography in 1880. Neither did they appear in the promotional materials used in their circus shows and exhibitions both nationally and abroad. Post–Civil War reconstruction was not exclusive to southern society and southern communities. Survivors of the bloodshed and social strife often sought to reconstruct their lives in the decades that followed. Bates was reportedly a "crabby type" who was often quick to anger and lash out, thereby getting into conflict with his neighbors and, occasionally, the law. The local constable even required Bates to post a peace bond, which was drawn down from complaints of damages and bodily injury from those who experienced the displeasure of the giant of Seville.[54]

The Civil War era was unfortunately replete with tales of similarly gruesome and violent acts, and many surviving victims and actors chose to put these events behind them. Some contemporary newspaper accounts suggested that Bates's loyalty returned to the Union, even after his notorious service to the Confederate cause. As reports of his marriage to Anna surfaced back in the states, his service record was remarkably reconstructed. A Hillsboro, Ohio newspaper that reported the wedding stated, "Captain Bates served his country with distinction during the late controversy and is in every respect a Union man of high standing."[55]

Other later accounts mentioned the captain's patriotism to the United States, although it's possible he was silent when there was celebration of the Union during Civil War reunions. In 1899, Seville hosted the sixth annual Medina County Soldiers and Sailors Reunion, where Anna Bates entertained everyone in song and then a welcoming speech. He did give a cheer to the returning Spanish-American War soldiers in attendance, but he was less vocal in cheering for the Union. At least he didn't wear his Confederate uniform.

While history may be written by the victors—and sometimes by the survivors—a person's conscience also demands quenching. It has been said that after the periods of mass trauma experienced during warfare, returning soldiers have often helped spark religious revivals. There is no

4441   FIRST BAPTIST CHURCH SEVILLE, OHIO.
ILLUSTRATED POST CARD CO., N. Y.

The Bates were members of First Baptist Church in Seville, Ohio, from the 1880s until their deaths. One pew was enlarged to accommodate the couple. *Authors collection.*

doubt that biblical teachings provided solace to many people following the trauma of the Civil War. Pastoral teachings from Colossians 3:13, "Forgive each other as Christ has forgiven you," would have provided some help in those regards, and they may have provided a shining light forward for a more peaceful and Christ-centered life. Although Bates was known for being a bit hard to get along with and short-tempered, even in his later years, his ferocious demeanor was apparently tempered by his wife and his religious convictions.

Captain Bates and Anna were conspicuously religious and were frequent attendees of the Seville Baptist Church. Bates married the church pastor's daughter Annette LaVonne Weatherby in 1900, twelve years after the death of his beloved Anna. She was a woman of normal stature, reportedly weighing a mere 135 pounds. They lived on the Bateses' farm until 1901, whereupon Bates sold off the farm and its stock, tools and crops, and they retired to their townhouse in the east end of Seville. He lived in Seville until his death on January 7, 1919.[56]

Medina County was in the middle of its second wave of Spanish (1918 H1N1) influenza infections when Martin Bates became ill. His official cause of death was listed as nephritis, a failure of the kidneys, with a contributing cause of arteriosclerosis. Nephritis and pneumonia were frequent complications of the Spanish flu and were often listed on the death certificates rather than the contributory virus. Perhaps the Seville giant succumbed to the deadly virus that infected 500 million people worldwide in four successive waves, worsened by his underlying health conditions. Maybe it took one of the deadliest pandemics in human history to strike down a giant among men. We will never know for sure, but it is possible that he fell victim to a virus that also killed an estimated 675,000 people in the United States alone. Throughout the country, newspapers ran short pieces to acknowledge the passing of Bates; unfortunately, they all too often ran with headlines like "Circus Freak Dies." Alas, the death of a mortal giant was maybe noteworthy as a curiosity, but as a possible victim to the Spanish flu, he was only one of the many.[57]

The Giants and an Educated, Caroling Bird

The Bateses reportedly had an "educated parrot with a fair singing voice" named Barnum. Captain Bates not only taught the parrot how to sing Christmas carols, like "Silent Night," and popular tunes, like "There'll Be a Hot Time in the Old Town Tonight," but he also taught it how to hum. According to newspaper reports, the parrot had a better than ordinary speaking voice and good memory, which frequently resulted in "playbacks" of family conversations to surprised visitors to the farm.

When Bates remarried and settled on his small property in Seville, he also taught the parrot to yell, "Get off my property!" when neighbors cut across his lawn. The parrot also learned to greet its mistress from its cage on the front porch. Supposedly, Barnum would occasionally accompany the Baptist church choir while Christmas caroling within the village. For the curious among you, the parrot sang baritone.[58]

Per the family's wishes, the funeral services were private, thus avoiding a crowd of "curiosity-seekers." Bates was buried in the family plot in Mound Hill Cemetery in Seville next to his beloved Anna in a coffin that was made to order well in advance of his death. When Anna had passed away years before, the Cleveland-based coffin maker had thought that the dimensions contained in the instructions were incorrect and had sent a coffin that was too small. Because of the mix-up, Anna was buried in a plain wooden box, despite the best intentions of the captain. Captain Bates didn't want the same issue to arise upon his eventual passing, so he paid to have his coffin constructed ahead of time. In order to avoid having it on public display, he bought it and stored it out of sight at home in his barn, prepared for the occasion of his eventual demise. Following the probate of his will, Annette LaVonne remained in town. She was active in her church and various Seville community organizations, including one in support of women's suffrage. After the captain's death, she reportedly promoted the registration of women voters in Medina County. She died in 1940 and was buried in Erie, Pennsylvania.[59]

THE START OF A RACE OF GIANTS?

Captain Bates and his first wife and fellow giantess, Anna, were not only experts on the subject of giants but were feared by some to be progenitors of a new race. The *Sheffield and Rotherham Independent* newspaper headline for the story on their wedding read, "Natural Selection." Amid its story about the wedding, the paper observed, "A London contemporary is concerned lest the trade of exhibiting giants and giantesses should suffer by the coupling of the great personages whose entrance together in holy matrimony we celebrate, since their example may be copied with the result of producing such swarms of young ones, that eight-foot men and women would cease to be a rarity." Translation: many people feared the union would create a race of giants, and given the theory Darwinism, maybe they would replace us diminutive mortals.[60]

There was an underlying concern from some when Anna was reportedly pregnant. Alas, their two children didn't live beyond birth, but both were sizable—18.00 pounds, twenty-four inches in length; and 23.75 pounds, thirty inches in length. A.P. Beach, MD, from Seville felt compelled to publicly report his role in the largest human birth on record to the nationally published *Medical Record* in 1879.

One New Orleans newspaper article headline suggested that Martin and Anna were "Pioneers in Human Development." The paper observed, "The Bates couple prove that colossal development is a possibility; it remains for scientists and philanthropists to find the way and the method." Sadly, with the early demise of their offspring, the Bates couple would no longer be the subject of public conjecture about a future race of giants.[61]

The average human height has gone up in industrialized countries over the last 150 years, and this is largely attributed to improved health, more and better food available to more people and, in general, a better quality of life. Humans have gotten, on average, four inches taller—not anywhere close to the two feet a Bates-like race of giants would measure up. Although subsequent individuals have been born who have claimed to be the tallest humans, the Bates couple remain the crowned champions of tallest couple and the largest live birth, that of their son.[62] Humanity it appears, will have to grow in other more desirable and beneficial ways than height if it wants to cultivate a "race of giants." In those regards, the Bates couple still holds a place in Medina County history in stimulating more civilized and cultured pursuits—an active church life and scientific farming—despite their challenging early years. After all, did they not also possess the hearts of giants?

8

FUN WITH FLAGS

Legacy of a Medina County Native

*H*ere are some interesting facts about the official flag of the State of Ohio:

- It has an official pledge very few people know about or ever recite.
- It is the only non-rectangular state flag in the United States.
- It is quite similar to the Cuban national flag, which was adopted by that government the same month and year as the Ohio flag.
- It was designed by a graduate of the University of Michigan.
- It was the state symbol introduced at a world event that is remembered primarily as the site of a national tragedy—the assassination of an Ohio-born president.

Given these facts, should the flag of the State of Ohio be treated with the same respect as the flag of the United States? Just as there is an etiquette for the treatment and retirement of Old Glory, the State of Ohio's flag is comparatively new and is relegated to a second-place honor in all official settings. Seventeen states across the nation possess official state flag pledges. In commemoration of the one hundredth anniversary of Ohio's flag, the 124th Ohio General Assembly adopted Amended SB 240, which established a pledge. Accordingly, the pledge to the state flag is simply: "I salute the flag of the State of Ohio and pledge to the Buckeye State respect and loyalty." Having attended many public meetings where the American flag is posted along with an Ohio flag, I have never heard this pledge—ever.

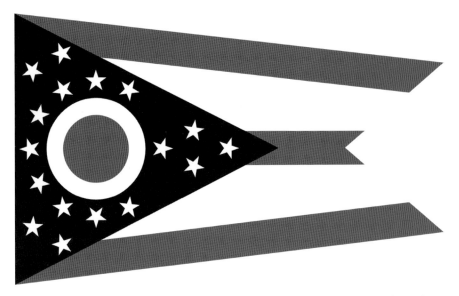

The official flag of the State of Ohio since 1902 was designed by a Michigan native and graduate of the University of Michigan. *Courtesy of the Ohio House of Representatives.*

In 2020, the 133rd Ohio General Assembly unanimously passed HB 32, which created an official ceremonial procedure in retiring an Ohio state flag, similar to the ceremony prescribed to the U.S. flag under state and federal law. The retirement ceremony spelled out in HB 32 added to the pledge a statement reminding everyone that it was born in the shadow of a national tragedy: "My first witness to our country as your state symbol was to the assassination of President William McKinley on September 14, 1901."

Ohio has a flag unlike any other state. It is the only state flag designed in the shape of a burgee, or a swallowtail pattern. Because of its shape, some say it was patterned from various Ohio regimental flags used during the Civil War, but others contend it also has a Cuban connection. After the United States seized Cuba from Spain during the Spanish-American War, the American Stars and Stripes flew there from January 1, 1899, until May 20, 1902. Thereupon, Cuba adopted a flag that closely resembles the Ohio flag.

The only Medina County native to be elected governor of the State of Ohio, George K. Nash, saw an opportunity for the Buckeye State to seize the spotlight at the Pan-American Exposition in 1901. It was a World's Fair that was held in Buffalo, New York, from May 1 to November 2, 1901. Since Ohio is the "mother of American presidents," many in Ohio wanted to showcase the state. Nash set up a commission to construct a big, fancy building at the Pan-American Exposition in honor of Ohio—and out front would wave Ohio's newly designed flag. Ohio's appropriation of $30,000 was expended mostly on the building, with its Grecian-style architecture and pure white appearance, which, according to one account, was "one of the finest and most admired on the ground." Of course, because of its shape and pedigree, the flag was the most distinctive.[63]

Both the building and the flag were designed by an engineer and architect from Cleveland, John Eisenmann. Born and raised in Michigan, he graduated from the University of Michigan in 1871 with a degree in civil engineering. He further studied architecture at the Polytechnics of Munich and Stuttgart. The growing industrial centers along the shores of Lake Erie offered second chances to many immigrants and emigrants in the 1880s, even those from the state up north.

Eisenmann was commissioned as the architect of the Cleveland Arcade and authored Cleveland's first comprehensive building code. He wanted to design a first-class building, but he also wanted a first-class and unique flag for the State of Ohio to fly in front of it. The assassination of McKinley at the event would add even more importance to memorializing Ohio's prominence.

On May 9, 1902, HB 213, under the sponsorship of W.S. McKinnon, speaker of the Ohio House of Representatives

MEDINA'S ONLY NATIVE SON ELECTED OHIO GOVERNOR: QUIET, EFFECTIVE AND STRICTEST INTEGRITY

Born in York Township, Nash is the only Medina County native to have ever been elected as the governor of the State of Ohio. Nash worked his way through higher education and entered Oberlin College at the age of twenty. In 1864, he enlisted as a private with Company K, 150th Ohio National Guard. Afterward studying law and passing the bar exam, he quickly rose to jurisprudential prominence and leadership within the Franklin County Republican Party. He was elected Franklin County prosecutor in 1870, despite the electoral advantages for Democrats in that county. Nash served as the Ohio attorney general (1880–1883) and served two terms as governor from 1900 to 1904. After his death in 1904, the *Marion Star* wrote, "He was a tireless worker and knew more of the details of the affairs of the state during his brief executiveship than has perhaps any other governor. His was a wonderfully successful administration, financially all during his term the treasury surplus grew, and he left the state with some $3,000,000 to the good."[64]

George K. Nash. *From* Biographical Cyclopedia and Portrait Gallery with an Historical Sketch of the State of Ohio, *vol. 1 (Cincinnati, OH: Western Biographical Publishing Company, 1883), 183.*

and member of the Ohio Pan-American Exposition Commission, the state officially adopted the flag. In memory of our slain president, who had waged the Spanish-American War that had freed Cuba, many saw it as a fitting resemblance. In addition, as was noted soon afterward, "A United States senator from Ohio introduced the resolution that made the people of Cuba free and independent. Ohio's sons rendered distinguished service on land and sea. An Ohio president conducted the Spanish-American War to a triumphant conclusion."[65]

Although it may not have the gloried past of the U.S. flag, the Ohio flag does have a connection to one of the most decisive wars in our history and a tragic presidential assassination, and it was designed to represent the hills, valleys, roads and waterways of the Buckeye State. The relatively new Ohio law answers the question: does it deserve similar prestige and respect afforded the American flag? Despite being designed by a Michigan native and graduate of the University of Michigan, perhaps the etiquette spelled out in HB 32 for the treatment and retirement of the flag will confirm that the only grudge we should hold is the one we hold on the college football field—perhaps not. Go Bucks!

9

THE 1908 MEDINA COUNTY VISIT
OF WILLIAM HOWARD TAFT

A Series of Unfortunate Events
for Acting Governor Harris

*I*n the earliest part of the twentieth century, a term like *hoodoo* or *skidoo* along with the number "23" became part of popular references to bad luck. When used together, these terms referred to being kicked out or a quick end to something. Unfortunately for Ohio governor Andrew L. Harris, an election-year newspaper story used the term *hoodoo* to suggest a quick end for someone was likely in relation to a controversial bill the governor had signed. A whistle-stop trip through Medina County in October 1908 by Republican presidential candidate William Howard Taft, along with Governor Harris, would add more to the tally of a series of unfortunate events that spelled a quick end in the long record of public service for the chief executive.

As the forty-fourth governor of Ohio, Andrew L. Harris was the last of the Civil War veterans to serve as the chief executive of our great state. He was a three-time elected lieutenant governor and rose from the rank of private to breveted brigadier general during the Civil War. While participating in eighteen battles, he was wounded twice—he was shot through the right arm at McDowell, Virginia, and through the left side at the Battle of Gettysburg. Harris overcame the permanent damage to his arm and pursued an active life overseeing scientific farming on five hundred acres in Preble County, and he had a notable law career.[66] He served in multiple local, county and state elected positions throughout his long career of public service. President William McKinley called him a "statesman of public recognition" and said he "was a soldier of exceptional gallantry."[67]

Harris became governor of the State of Ohio when Governor John M. Pattison passed away six months into his term of office as lieutenant governor on June 18, 1906. Harris became the second person in Ohio's history to become governor after the death of the chief executive. The first lieutenant governor to succeed after a death of the elected governor only served for five uneventful months, but Harris was not so lucky to have such an insipid term.[68]

One of the major problems for Andrew L. Harris was that he was not of the same party as Governor Pattison. Lieutenant governors were elected separately at the time. Immediately, stories in Democratic Party papers and from leaders of the loyal opposition referred to him as the acting governor. Of course, the Republican-leaning press and elected officials clearly contended that he was the governor of the State of Ohio with the full executive and appointing authority that his predecessor had possessed. Publicly reminded by the partisan press of his ascension by virtue of death and not by voter approval, Governor Harris's appointments and decisions were frequent targets. It was an easy target for the Democrats to claim he was only the acting governor since the lieutenant governor position remained vacant from June 18, 1906, to January 11, 1909. Some newspaper reports claimed that he was both governor and lieutenant governor at the same time, further clouding the issue.[69]

Among the many contentious laws passed in his term, the Rose County Local Option Law became the most critical issue for Governor Harris to weather. Regrettably, he had to tackle it in an election year that would have been straightforward for most Ohio Republicans.[70] The Rose County Local Option Law provided that "35 percent of qualified electors of any county might petition the commissioners or any judge of such county for a local election to determine whether or not intoxicating liquors should be sold within the county." It went into effect on September 1, 1908, and before the end of the year, sixty-two of the state's eighty-eight counties voted to go dry, closing 1,902 saloons. To add a bit of confusion, under the law, dry towns in a county that voted to remain wet were still dry, but wet towns in counties that voted to go dry were required to close their saloons.[71]

In a small headline, the *Dayton Herald* ominously warned, "Rose Bill Has Hoodoo '23.'" It explained, "The Rose County Local Option Measure is the twenty-third bill to be signed by Governor Harris, and whether or not this numerical designation is an evil omen for the law or the saloon is yet to be shown. To the average dispenser of liquid balm, however, this 'skidoo' sign carries with it no assurance of hope."[72] It proved to be an ominous sign for the unelected governor.

Governor Harris had always been on the side of the Anti-Saloon League and other temperance forces, but many questioned why such contentious issues had to be given to the voters amid a presidential and gubernatorial election. The *Medina County Gazette* offered, after the 1908 general election, that it cost Governor Harris thousands of votes and contended that it was political folly not to have delayed these elections until later.[73]

PRESIDENTIAL CAMPAIGN TRIP TO MEDINA

On the morning of Tuesday, October 13, 1908, a national presidential campaign swung through northeast Ohio, featuring Republican candidate Vice President William Howard Taft. Often referred to as Judge Taft, this Ohio native was conducting the whistle-stop campaign trip on the back of a passenger railroad car against his Democratic rival, two-time nominee William Jennings Bryan.

A headline in the *Norwalk Reflector* read, "Taft Speaks to Thousands." It describes how Judge Taft made fourteen addresses in a whistle-stop campaign sweep through northeast Ohio, traveling through six congressional districts and seven counties in a circuitous pattern from Lake Erie to the Ohio River. Because of a derailment in a car transfer between the Erie to the B&O in Sterling, just south of Seville, the Taft group pulled into Wadsworth twenty minutes late and was greeted by a crowd of over five thousand residents, workmen and schoolchildren.

After giving a detailed speech on how the Republican Party was the friend of labor, "Mr. Taft presented Governor Harris. Cheers filled the air. He greeted the people and was just starting to talk when the train started." Being late in a presidential whirlwind campaign is certainly not out of the ordinary or largely considered unfortunate. However, Harris was cut off in the middle of a speech to constituents in a tough campaign against pro-saloon voters. This too brief encounter for Governor Harris in the Wadsworth visit was just another small sign of his ongoing struggle—if not a humbling experience.

There are no reports of what the Harris aides said to the Taft people, but at least at the next stop, such an ignominious and abrupt ending to the governors' speech would not happen again. At the next engagement, while they were only able to remain in town for a scarce ten minutes, Medina greeted the presidential candidate and entourage with a grand parade—a half mile long—the Knights of Pythias band heading the procession. An

When William Howard Taft stopped at the train depot in Medina on his northeast Ohio presidential campaign tour, the *Norwalk Daily Reflector* reported three thousand people attended. *Author's collection.*

estimated three thousand people crowded around the depot to hear Judge Taft for a short bit and even briefer comments from Governor Harris. It appears by all accounts that the Medina event, regardless of its brevity, at least allowed the governor to complete his address before taking off along the tracks.[74]

Despite running a vigorous campaign, Bryan suffered the worst loss in his three presidential campaigns. Taft won by a comfortable margin nationwide: 321 to 162 electoral voters and a popular vote of 7,678,908 to 6,409,104. In Ohio, Taft won with 572,312 or 51.03 percent of the vote, while Bryan obtained 502,721 votes or 44.82 percent of the total. Governor Harris won in Medina County by a majority of 1,019 votes.[75] As a local sympathetic press reported, "The saloonists of Wadsworth jumped into politics against Gov. Harris and F.W. Woods. That's the last element that Medina County wants to see in its politics, and it won't stand for it now or ever. A great majority of Republicans and Democrats agree on that point."[76]

Despite the concerns of the experienced Republican campaign managers, the gubernatorial race was framed around Republican Harris's pro-temperance forces versus the Democrat Judson Harmon's accusations of state corruption. Hinting at a "divide and conquer" strategy, the *Defiance Daily Crescent* questioned, "In the country, Harris talks dry, and in the cities, the Republican machines talk wet. Will any Democrat be fooled by such tactics?"[77] Harris relied heavily on the anti-saloon sentiment in his campaign speeches, as he was being frequently lambasted for the inconsistency of the Republican candidates in the cities by the strategic campaign tactics of the Personal Liberty League, funded by the saloons and alcohol interests across the state.[78]

The anti-saloon strategy mostly worked in Medina County—except for very pro-wet voters in Liverpool Township. However, in statewide results, Governor Andrew L. Harris lost to Judge Harmon by a plurality of 19,372 votes. Of the state Democratic ticket, only the governor and the treasurer of state—by a slim plurality of 1,431 votes—were elected, while all the remaining statewide Republican office seekers won by large majorities, ranging from 54,000 to 19,000 votes.[79]

"Hoodoo 23" of the Rose Law indeed became a bad omen for acting governor Harris. Being cut off mid-speech in front of a presumably favorable crowd in Wadsworth would, at worst, be a mild irritation to the normally genial candidate. Similarly, it was just a small incident in a series of unfortunate events for an ill-fated campaign to elect a noble and aged public servant in an election year predominately favorable to Republicans statewide.

Newspapers and historians alike reflected that Harris and the temperance issue incorporated in the Rose Law were ahead of the public. The cause of local, statewide and then national Prohibition would continue to grow. Over the decade, the Prohibition movement, so prominent in Medina County politics, would find much more widespread support nationwide. The acts of political courage and conscience by Governor Harris in 1908 would prove to be premature to the political sentiment of most voters. As I have been told regarding elected politics, it is far better to leave the day before the voters want to get rid of you than the day after. Timing is everything.

10

ANOTHER YEAR IN OFFICE

1905 Constitutional Amendment Increased Terms of State Politicians but Created the Even-Odd Years Election Cycle

L ike many state constitutions written in the first decades of our grand republic, the first Ohio Constitution stands as a prime example of Jeffersonian influence and design. As historian Daniel J. Ryan noted over a century ago:

> *It distinctly bears the impress of Thomas Jefferson and was intended to be the foundation of a people's government. The executive was ignored and restricted, the Judiciary controlled and limited, and all the power was placed in the legislature, which was elected for a short period.*[80]

To that end, the general assembly was elected annually and held sessions annually. As the theory went, the power of government, when largely placed in the hands of the legislature, was best comprised of "citizen" legislators. Ideally, they would be held accountable to the voters annually. Advocates often referenced the "educational influence of frequent campaigns."

Ohio house speaker William G. Batchelder III told me once that the State of Ohio is more often safer when the general assembly is not in session. As a conservative, he often spoke with skepticism about the power of government and the influence of special interests. This viewpoint derived from his many years of service in the Ohio House is understandable and, for many of us, shared. Regardless, the historical trend since our founding is one of increasing the concentration of power in the hands of the elected officials, not one of deferring it very often to the voters. Elected officials in Ohio, as well as those in other states, have, over the decades, lengthened their terms of office as much as the public can generally tolerate. Voter fatigue, even now, is all too common and often recognized as a shortcoming of the democratic process.

Over the years, the various state constitutions that originally incorporated those thresholds on legislative bodies were amended to require biennial elections rather than annual ones. By 1904, thirty-three states had biennial elections, while only eleven had annual elections. But the journeys of those states from annual to biennial elections were often fraught with vigorous debate. Similarly, they coincided with a bit of confusion over the necessary frequency of elections for other elected officials.

Delegates to the Ohio Constitutional Convention of 1850 sought to remedy the short terms of office for the general assembly, as well as the unfettered dominance they had over the judiciary and executive branches under the existing Jeffersonian-framed constitution. Once it was ratified by the voters on June 19, 1851, the terms of the house of representatives and Ohio Senate members were limited to two years rather than one. In the special election on June 19, 1851, Medina County voters cast 1,853 to 1,291 (59 percent) ballots in favor of the new constitution, while statewide, it was a little bit closer, with 125,564 yeas versus 109,276 nays, or 53 percent approval.[81]

Under the new 1851 Ohio Constitution, the voters would also elect, in odd numbered years, a governor, lieutenant governor, secretary of state, treasurer and attorney general for terms of two years and the state auditor for four years. Although Ohio had technically adopted a biennial election, various other elected offices were out of sync with one another and with the federal elections held every even year. To complicate the election cycles further, over the years, other elected terms of offices were created by the general assembly, and varying terms of election were established. Ohio township trustees had three-year terms, and county officials had three- or four-year terms, depending on the office. By 1904, Ohio township and municipal officials were also being selected in the spring, not in fall elections. Election confusion was evident, and the frequency was unappreciated.[82]

Many started to voice opinions in favor of adjust the timing and frequency of elections. Newspaper editorials, politicians, businessmen and many others complained. As a *Cleveland Plain Dealer* headline argued: "Too Many Elections." In 1886, the paper opined on the issue:

> *At the present time, we have two annual elections—in the spring and in the fall. Each is expensive in its way. After each new candidate begin to lay plans which they hope to see consummated a year later. Thus politics*

and political motives rule from year's end to year's end. In view of the continuous wrangle and planning to achieve office and the interminable buttonholing and setting up of political pins, would it not be better were state officers elected to four-year terms and county and township officers to serve two or four years, as the importance of the office may determine, with biennial elections held at the same time that state and national elections are now held, in November of each alternate year?[83]

A constitutional convention held in 1873–74 sent to Ohio voters another rewritten constitution that made significant changes to the powers of the general assembly and the governor. In addition, it proposed biennial elections on the Tuesday succeeding the first Monday in November. Similarly, it established four-year terms for county officials but left the legislature in charge of determining the number and term limits of township and municipal officials. The voters decided on August 18, 1874, that they were unequivocally against its adoption, with 250,169 opposing and only 102,885 voters, or 29 percent, favoring it. The results in Medina County were no better, with 874 in favor and 2,248 opposed—only 28 percent were favorable to the proposed new constitution.[84]

In 1889, another attempt was made to adopt biennial elections for state and county officers in even years, while township and elected municipal officials would be elected in November of odd years. In November of that year, 257,663 Ohio voters favored the constitutional amendment, and 254,215 opposed it. While it passed among a majority of the voters who were actually voting on the issue, it didn't legally pass. The Ohio Supreme Court ruled in December that year, that the Ohio Constitution required passage by a majority of the voters casting ballots at that election. In other words, the amendment received a majority of the votes cast for it but not a majority of the general vote.[85]

Resolving the frequency of elections and the varying terms of office would require a major adjustment in extending terms of office for many elected officials throughout the state. If asked, most citizens would probably prefer that many politicians stay in office a very short time rather than grant them an additional year in office without facing another election. But in 1905, the Ohio voters cast ballots to increase by one year the terms of office for a number of politicians—actually affecting political offices from top to bottom.

In 1905, by a total of 702,699 yeas and only 90,762 nays, there was overwhelming support to change when state officeholders faced election and set up a pattern of even- and odd-year elections in November. In Medina County, the vote was 3,675 yeas to only 801 nays. It was a single amendment, not a dramatic rewrite of the constitution. It passed in every community except one: Homer Township. The governor, lieutenant governor, Ohio senators and representatives, the state treasurer, attorney general and some state supreme court justices were to be elected on a uniform biennial basis.[86]

As Judge William H. West, an Ohio Supreme Court justice, former state attorney general and twelve-year member of the general assembly, explained at the time, "I believe that the third section of the amendment continues in office every elective officer of the state holding office when the amendment was adopted, until a successor to him shall be elected at an election held after the adoption of, and under, the amendment."[87]

To permanently fix the problem of too-frequent elections and uneven terms of office, regular elections for state and county offices would occur in the even years to coincide with federal elections, while local office elections would occur in the odd years. The result was not only a one-time and one-year extension for terms of office for those already in office, but it was the establishment of a pattern of general elections in Ohio that has persisted to this day.

Federal and state regular elections now occur in even years—presidential and gubernatorial election years—and they outperform in voter turnout than so-called local elections for school board members, municipal court and township and municipal officials in odd numbered years. This cyclical pattern of voter turnout persists. The highest turnout is seen during presidential elections; gubernatorial is in the middle, and local are lowest. As depicted in the table opposite, for the entire state of Ohio, the typical up and down cycle of voter turnout and interest is irrespective of region and county.

Those who favored this change were party leaders, business owners, newspaper editors and elected officials, like Ohio governors William McKinley, George K. Nash and Myron Herrick. Those who opposed it were primarily organized labor organizations and their supporters—other than a few conservative editors who argued on behalf of regular and annual accountability of legislators to the electorate.[88]

Other states, like Iowa and Massachusetts, underwent similar debates over the issue and provided similar reasons for adopting or opposing biennial elections. In 1896, Raymond L. Bridgman, a prolific author, political observer and eventual president of the Massachusetts State House Press Association, summarized the argument for the changes to biennial elections.

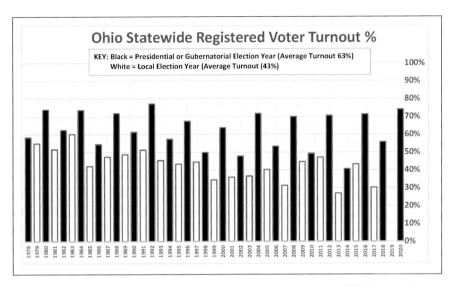

The statewide registered voter turnout from 1978 to 2020. *Courtesy of the Ohio Secretary of State.*

He stated, "The admitted evils of the present system, concisely stated, are, first, incessant political agitation; second, overmuch legislation; third, instability and uncertainty in the laws; fourth, unnecessary and wasteful expenditure of money."[89]

Iowa state senator G.M. Titus's arguments in a 1904 forum stated briefly what many were saying in Ohio at the time: "The best statemen of the country endorse the idea; that 'we have too much politics,' the biennial elections would cut expenses, that an 'off year' election is not an educator; that states which have adopted the idea are pleased with it and would not return to the old system."[90] Evidently, Ohio voters agreed a year later, and the pattern of up in even years and down in odd years began and persists well over one hundred years later. However, many might argue we still have too much politics, despite the change—but for entirely different reasons than those from over a century ago.

11

FRANK W. WOODS

A Local Bull Moose and Father
of Ohio Public Utilities Commission

*F*rank W. Woods, a Chatham Township native and prominent Medina attorney, served in the Ohio House of Representatives in the seventy-seventh and seventy-eighth sessions (1906–10) and was elected to the Fourth Ohio Constitutional Convention (1912). Prior to being elected to the house, he served as a Medina County prosecuting attorney from 1900 to 1904. In the general assembly, he caucused with the Republican Party, but he was an adversary to some of the big city political machines and business syndicates that were prevalent at the time.

His notable success was in the general assembly from 1906 to 1910. As a legislator, he authored the early measure to regulate the rates charged by public utility corporations. Contemporary Ohio newspaper accounts referred to him as the "father" of the Ohio Public Utilities Commission. The legislation also sought to abolish all special taxing boards, creating a new board of three members with control over public service corporations, power to levy taxes, ability to prevent watering of stock and other dramatic powers. Like any major reform at the time, it would take several legislative sessions and changes to the Ohio Constitution to enact even modest oversight of a very powerful business interest—public utilities.

His participation in the 1912 Ohio Constitutional Convention was in keeping with his progressive political views on Prohibition, the regulation of businesses, the elimination of capital punishment and uniform taxation. On the suffrage issues, however, he was not personally in favor of women's suffrage. "I am one of the members who voted to submit the woman's suffrage proposal to the state. Personally, I am against woman's suffrage. I do not intend to vote for it on election day, but I am willing for the people of the state to say whether they want it. Now, I do not want to vote for that, but I do want to vote to take that word 'white' out of the constitution. I think it is ridiculous that a state like Ohio in 1912 should have that word in its constitution."[91] The women's suffrage issue passed in Medina County by 51.0 percent, while the removal of the word *white* also handily passed with 66.0 percent of the vote. Statewide, both measures failed, with 57.4 percent opposed to women's suffrage and 52.3 percent opposed to removing the reference to *white* from the Ohio Constitution.

Woods also zealously advocated for a uniform classification of property for the purposes of imposing taxes. During that period of Ohio history, there was a constant battle in the general assembly over taxation. Historically and according to Ohio law, general property tax was supposed to be applied equally. In an agrarian economy, taxes based on property values of buildings and land is relatively easy to see, understand and determine. However, other forms of wealth, such as mortgages, stocks, bonds and other intangible property was more difficult to tax equally or, as many business interests argued, fairly. The transition in the state of Ohio to a modern commercial and industrial giant undermined the principles of taxation that had been applied to farms and commercial structures. Frank W. Woods sided with those advocating for a tax system in which businesses and the wealthy would have to pay their share of the tax burden, in other words, a system devoid of classifications that exempted certain types of wealth. During a long debate on taxation on May 1, 1912, he summarized his opposition to classification of taxes: "Well, if anybody pays less under classification, somebody will pay more. If you let one class out for less than it is now taxed, somebody will have to pay that additional burden."[92]

In 1912, as a member of the Teddy Roosevelt wing of the party, he split and joined the Bull Moose "Progressive Party." That year, he ran for the U.S. Congress in the newly organized Progressive Party. Although he won Medina County by a sizable margin, he lost in the remaining part of the Twentieth District. This pattern was seen elsewhere in the state due to the division of Republican voters. The Democrat challenging the Republican congressional incumbent won the district that year.

In 1914, Woods also ran for Ohio secretary of state, again with the Progressive Party. Again, he lost—this time by a considerable margin. The Progressive Party had a measurable impact in Medina County and the statewide races in 1912— mainly benefiting all the Democrats because of the split of the Republicans. Two years later, however, it was a marginal minor political party and barely outperformed the Socialists. Eventually, Frank W. Woods would find his way back to the local Republican Party but never rose again in elected public office. In 1917, he was appointed chairman of the Medina County committee in charge of promoting and selling the thrift and war savings stamps in the earliest part of the war. Later in the war, he provided help on many occasions to promote efforts for Liberty Bond subscriptions throughout the county. After the war, he ran in the 1920 Ohio Republican primary to become a presidential delegate in the Fourteenth Congressional District for Leonard Wood, but he lost out to the Harding machine delegates. He was ever faithful to the progressive Teddy Roosevelt wing of the Republican Party, and he was a patriot.

After his reported death in 1927 at the age of fifty-four, newspapers throughout the state commented that he was an "honest and sincere man." Upon his demise, the *Columbus Dispatch* headline called him a "former state Solon." (Solon was an ancient Greek Athenian statesman and lawmaker remembered for his efforts to legislate against political, economic and moral decline.) To that end, Frank W. Woods was a skilled attorney, lawmaker and persistent advocate for progressive causes locally, statewide and nationally. According to the *Cincinnati Enquirer* at the time of his death, Woods, after the 1914 loss for the office of the secretary of state, "had taken only a small part in politics, never apparently having become sympathetic to the style of game played by the rejuvenated Republican Party." The "return to normalcy" and the Roaring Twenties of the Harding/Coolidge era just wasn't going to get active support from a die-hard Progressive Bull Moose, especially someone like Frank W. Woods.

12

WADSWORTH THREATENS TO DETACH FROM MEDINA COUNTY

Breaking Up Is Always Hard to Do

Back in 1840, when the general assembly created Summit County and detached the townships of Richfield, Bath, Copley and Norton from Medina County, a solid argument could have been made that they should have included Wadsworth as well. After all, the roads westward to Seville and northwest to Medina, the county seat, were reportedly dismal and precarious, especially during the wet months of the year. Particularly, the road to Medina, the county seat, traversed a rather inhospitable terrain. As the *History of the Western Reserve* relates:

> *The early surveyors named the western part of Wadsworth, because of its swampy condition, "the Infernal Regions," and the sluggish stream that oozed through the swamps was named "River Styx." This part of the township was dreaded by the early traveler.*[93]

In contrast, the east and west highway traversed much easier ground and was laid out in 1808, before the township received its first settlers.[94] There was regular commerce and travel eastward to the settlements of Western Star, Norton Center, Johnsons' Corners and New Portage (it later became Barberton). The latter was a direct connection to the Ohio & Erie Canal at the mouth of Wolff Creek. The Ohio & Erie Canal was completed to New Portage in 1827 and Clinton in 1828. In 1827, the price of a bushel of wheat that a local farmer could get jumped from five cents to one dollar almost overnight. For farmers in Wadsworth, the road to prosperity and commerce appeared to move eastward, nowhere close to the county seat.[95]

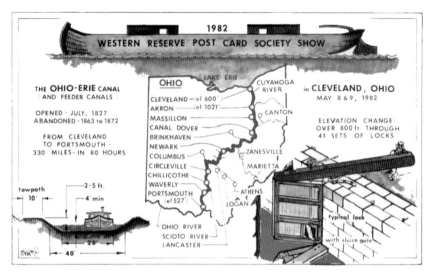

A 1982 Western Reserve Society Show postcard depicting the Ohio and Erie Canal System that transformed Ohio from having a subsistence, cashless pioneer farming economy to a cash-rich market-based agricultural economy. *Author's collection.*

Transportation links helped local farmers and the services they used to mill wood and grain, like the Wadsworth Milling Company. Postcard dated 1907. *Author's collection.*

The Ohio & Erie Canal was the interstate highway of the 1830s; through it traveled all commercial and passenger vessels from the southeast corner of Medina County. After all, Norton Township was a part of Medina County since the very beginning of the county, and as commercial traffic grew and as farmers profited from the direct connection to the markets in the east, so did the entry of new settlers. Wadsworth grew from a population of 965 in 1830 to 1,481 in 1840 and then 1,703 in 1860—much of it helped by the Ohio & Erie Canal connection to the east. Additional commercial and population growth that would later be attributed to steam railroads did not come until after 1861, when the Atlantic & Great Western Railroad was completed to the area.

Near the bustling traffic along the Ohio & Erie Canal, the little communities in the area thrived. A large branch of the Church of Jesus Christ of Latter-day Saints organized and settled in New Portage in the early 1830s. Their founder, Joseph Smith, visited New Portage on several occasions. The commercial and social links were located primarily to the east of Wadsworth, not west nor northwest to the county seat. The roads and the canal—essential transportation links for commercial traffic—kept the Wadsworth farmers, merchants and fledgling industries tied to the east. Regardless of what might have been a logical and uncontroversial decision at the time, the general assembly kept Wadsworth as part of Medina County. This was not the end of the story, as it was revisited several decades later.

Proposed Detachment from Medina County

A significant community-driven desire to detach Wadsworth came in 1911. Area newspapers covered an effort to detach Wadsworth and annex it to Summit County. In February of that year, Wadsworth chamber president A.W. Breyley indicated that many in town, including himself, were very favorable to the proposition. He stated that roads in that direction were better, that the payment of taxes and court business was better handled in Akron than in Medina and that "the people of Wadsworth would get better business protection they claim in this county than in Medina."[96] He predicted that petitions to that effect would be circulated soon.

The initiative grew along with grievances against Medina County commissioners throughout that year. In January 1912, the *Akron Beacon Journal* reported that citizens were accusing the county of withholding its rightful share of state aid for public highways. The feelings of dissatisfaction

Wadsworth residents benefitted greatly from a speedy and affordable access to Akron and beyond. When connected in April 1907, it provided passenger service at first hourly and in then thirty-minute headways to the Akron area. The Northern Ohio Traction and Light Company (NOT&L), headquartered in Akron, was the largest and, by some contemporary accounts, the finest electric railway system in Northeast Ohio. In its heyday, it owned more than 250 route miles that connected Cleveland, Akron, Canton, Massillon, New Philadelphia, Kent and Ravenna in a network of high-speed transportation, as shown below. At the same time, the NOT&L transported three times the number of passengers that its closest rivals, the Lake Shore Electric and the Cleveland, Southwestern & Columbus Electric Railway, transported.[97]

A Northern Ohio Traction interurban car in Downtown Wadsworth Park. *Author's collection.*

were so intense that the newspaper predicted that at least 90 percent of the citizens would sign a petition to annex the territory to Summit County. The Wadsworth Chamber of Commerce, village officials and the township trustees jointly chimed in that if an appeal to the county commissioners did not result in their fair share of road funds that petitions would be circulated at once. They asserted, "When the question is put to the vote of the people, it is predicted that it will pass by the largest majority ever given to any other measure which has been presented to the citizens."[98]

Akron merchants, like M. O'Neil of the O'Neil Company; C.H. Yeager, president of the Yeager Company; and Don A. Goodwin owner of the Buchtel Hotel, were unsurprisingly in favor of the move, citing benefits to Akron as well as Wadsworth.[99] Wadsworth even had a speedy connection to Barberton, a distance of six miles, and eventually Akron via the Northern Ohio Traction and Light, which opened on April 9, 1907. At the opening

This Northern Ohio Traction & Light Company (NOT&L) system map connected Wadsworth to the major industrial cities of Northeast Ohio. *This map is from the author's dissertation.*

celebration of the line extension, Wadsworth Village mayor R.L. Johnson, Akron mayor Charles Kempel and other dignitaries predicted the speedy connection would be a mutual benefit to both communities and would prove to be one of the most beneficial improvements in Wadsworth's history. In a short time, passenger train service on the half-hour to the Akron area would improve the connection to Summit County, as well as Cleveland and Canton, and help affirm those sentiments.[100]

So, the move to detach and annex Wadsworth was all about roads and rail transportation? Maybe this was the case in part, but there was apparently another important issue: the legal sale of alcohol. In a February 23, 1911 *Akron Beacon Journal* headline, Wadsworth Mayor Ault explained, "Impetus to Join Summit Is Thirst." He observed that many in the community were still upset when all of Medina County became "dry" under what was called the Rose Law, despite Wadsworth voting in favor of remaining "wet."[101]

The Wadsworth Village area was the home of a large labor element. The *Akron Times-Democrat* related in 1902, "Beer and tobacco are as much of a commodity with this class as coffee and sugar. Where the laboring classes control the balance of elective power, saloons will remain undisturbed, and the temperance people will have to do a little educating before they undertake to force a vote on the liquor issue."[102] The local option vote in 1902 for Wadsworth was a conclusive victory for the "wets" and defeat for the "drys." But within a few years and with changes in the state law, the temperance forces tried again, this time with a countywide approach called the Rose Local Option Law that would drown out the "wets."

In December 1908, the entire county voted by a majority of 1,204 to ban the sale of alcohol. Reportedly, "As a result of the vote, six saloons will be closed in Wadsworth and one in Liverpool." In that year, because of the Rose Law, sixty-two counties in the state went entirely dry, and nine voted to remain wet. Summit County was a decidedly "wet" county, and many in Wadsworth no doubt had a strong thirst to legally purchase alcohol.[103]

By May 1912, the drive and thirst to detach Wadsworth were finally being addressed in Medina and Columbus. Regarding roads, the *Akron Beacon Journal* headline said it all: "Chamber of Commerce Scores Great Victory: Succeeds in Getting State Aid for Wadsworth from County Commissioners— Other Improvements are Well Under Way."[104] At the same time that county commissioners were winning back their Wadsworth constituents to the Medina County fold, the issue of Prohibition and the movement toward local options were making their way through the statewide political system. The Rose Law was on the way to being revised. Likewise, the village option under the Beal Law was being enhanced by home rule proposals during the Ohio Constitutional Convention debates in which this was a very hot topic. Progressive Republican Frank Woods was elected to represent the county in the Ohio Constitutional Convention and spoke eloquently of the need for maintaining local options. There was considerable debate over a constitutional amendment that would allow the statewide licensing of alcohol while preserving the various local options.[105]

At the special election on September 3, 1912, Ohio voters overwhelmingly approved the amendment by 59.1 percent, creating a system of licensing for the sale of alcohol; in Medina County, 647 voters favored the licensing scheme while 562 opposed it.[106] At the same time, Medina County's results for Proposition No. 6, the Initiative and Referendum Delegation of Authority to the People of Ohio, adopted in 1912, was 595 in favor to 341 opposed. Thereafter, given the first opportunity for Ohio citizens to submit initiative petitions calling on the general assembly to enact new laws in the upcoming session, three of the five laws concerned liquor law enforcement. As the *Akron Beacon Journal* observed, the petition filings with the secretary of state "marks the formal opening of another bitter legislative war between the 'wets' and 'drys.'"[107]

Because of the home rule provision in the newly modified Ohio Constitution, the *Medina Sentinel* warned the county residents to "get ready for saloons."[108] However, when Wadsworth Village was finally able to vote under the Beal Law in December 1914, the majority vote total was 136 in favor of staying "dry," despite the efforts of a local Beal Law Committee conducted by a businessmen's committee.[109] In short order, no longer driven by a bad roads issue or a thirst for saloons in the community, it seems that Wadsworth's businesses and citizens abandoned the detachment issue and presumably drove over better roads sober.

TALLY-HO TO LODI'S TAYLOR INN

"The Comforts of a City with the Quiet of the Country"

*I*n the first decade of the twentieth century, men of wealth and property sought the thrill of motoring around the countryside. Early manufacturers of automobiles were abundant throughout northeast Ohio. Cleveland was replete with a great number of industrialists, bankers, financiers and promising inventors that helped make the city a prominent leader in automobile production, and it was full of enthusiasts. According to Derek Moore with the Crawford Auto and Aviation Museum at the Western Reserve Historical Society, between 1896 and 1907, Cleveland produced the most automobiles in America. It mostly specialized in high-quality and luxury cars.[110]

In those early days of the motoring sport being promoted by Cleveland enthusiasts, Taylor Inn was a reported favorite spot for dinner and an overnight stay. In downtown Lodi, it was built across from what the *1897 Atlas and Directory of Medina County* identified as a "Hexagon Square." It was the crossroads of major highways to Medina, Mansfield, Wooster, Elyria and a relatively passable roadway from the Barberton/Akron area. The village likewise had passenger and freight stations for the Wheeling & Lake Erie and Baltimore & Ohio Railroads just south of downtown. It was a perfect meeting place of historical trails, local dirt roads, diversely improved regional highways and interstate steam railway systems.[111]

The hostel was built in 1898 by prominent local banker and businessman A.B. Taylor for $80,000 as a memorial to his father. It quickly became one of the finest hotels in Ohio and a popular resort for the region's wealthiest

The Tally-Ho Car Rally by the Cleveland Automobile Club to Taylor Inn, circa 1903. The automobiles featured were Winton motor carriages and White motor vehicles, which were manufactured in Cleveland. *Author's collection.*

people. Comprising thirty guest rooms, it was described as "first-class city accommodations—cleanly, pretty rooms, with bathrooms, billiard room, electricity—anything and everything that could or would be required."[112] It included a large lobby with marble floors and wainscotting, a parlor adorned with fireplaces and mantels, a dedicated barbershop, bowling alleys and a tennis court.[113]

Unfortunately, the Panic of 1893, followed by the Panic of 1896, led to one the nation's worst depressions to that date, affecting the spending habits of even the wealthiest. The business activity of the venture, even as the effects of the depression waned in 1898, could not bear the cost of this grandeur, and Taylor was forced to liquidate. Locals referred to it as "Taylor's Folly," a taunting somewhat motivated by the demolition of a popular Bailey's Hotel at the same location.[114]

Taylor offered it to Western Reserve University and then Oberlin College; the latter took it over in 1901 but sold it in 1918 to private owners. Between those years, it was sometimes called the "white elephant" of Oberlin College. Regardless, many wealthy travelers enjoyed its opulence and first-class accommodations away from the smoke and grime of industry expanding in Cleveland, Akron and Lorain. After new owners took over the venture in 1918, the surge of the oil and gas industry in western Medina County led to a huge uptick in business, but these guests were nothing like the upscale customers of the early 1900s.

The regional economy had largely rebounded after 1900, and the region's wealthy families started to venture out from the central industrial cities on a regular basis. Located less than a day's journey from Cleveland or Akron, the Taylor Inn of Lodi hosted many of the region's wealthiest and prominent families. For example, on October 11, 1903, the society news section of the

The Lodi Taylor Inn, 1916. *Author's collection.*

Cleveland Plain Dealer related visitations of such Cleveland notables as Mr. and Mrs. Liberty Dean Holden and Mr. and Mrs. Alvah Stone Chisholm Sr., accompanied by Akron businessman Mr. Lucius Bierce Lyman and his socialite wife and Medina native Emma Laverne (Bishop) Lyman. Liberty D. Holden was the son of Liberty E. Holden, a Cleveland real estate investor and owner of the *Plain Dealer* and the renowned Hollenden Hotel. Alvah Stone was also a prominent industrialist and financier. The region's wealthiest families appreciated and enjoyed the first-class accommodations provided by the Taylor Inn; this, of course, was aided by the adventure of a motoring trip in the new-fangled inventions of the emerging age of the automobile. These automobilists, as they liked to call themselves, were the wealthiest and most socially prominent people in the region, and the Taylor Inn of Lodi was often a sought-after waystation on their automobile adventures.[115]

The Cleveland Automobile Club was formed in 1900 to promote driving as a sport, but it also helped the industry. Likewise, it promoted "gentlemanly" standards of behavior and etiquette on roadways used by horses. Years later, it also pushed for a "good-roads" agenda in the state legislature. The club conducted regular weekend motoring across the countryside, weather permitting.

The club was the second such organization formed in the nation, and it is the oldest automobile club remaining. In addition, it sponsored competitive

The Hollenden is located close to "Automobile Row" where all of the leading makers are represented. There are numerous dependable garages in the vicinity. The Headquarters of the Cleveland Automobile Club is in the Hotel Lobby and the Tourist will find the fullest possible information cheerfully placed at his disposal.

The... Beautiful **TAYLOR INN**
LODI, OHIO
40 MILES FROM CLEVELAND
The Comforts of a City with the Quiet of the Country
PURE AIR, GOOD WATER, NO SMOKE, NO DIRT
For Descriptive Booklet and terms, address,
H.K. ARMSTRONG
LODI, OHIO

Left: An advertisement in the 1915 AAA Blue Book for Motorists featuring the Hollenden Hotel and the home of the Cleveland Automobile Club. *From* The Official Automobile AAA Blue Book: A Touring Hand-Book of the Principal Automobile Routes in the Central States, 15th Year *(Chicago: Automobile Blue Book Publishing Company, 1915).*

Above: A re-creation of a July 19, 1903 *Plain Dealer* advertisement promoting the attractive merits of the Taylor Inn of Lodi and targeting the wealthy who were seeking refuge from the dirt and grime of industrialized Cleveland. *Image created by the author.*

races for manufacturers to promote their newest innovations in automobile technology to the wealthy enthusiasts. The very beginnings of our emerging "car culture" involved track and road races for inventors to continuously improve the vehicles and to encourage the development of driving skills over rough roadways.[116]

Attesting to the early premise that motoring was actually a rough sport requiring skill and practice, the standards and expectations for a pleasant trip have certainly changed over the last century. The *Cleveland Plain Dealer* reported on May 25, 1903, that a previous Saturday trip promoted by the Cleveland Automobile Club from Cleveland, Cuyahoga Falls, Akron, Barberton and Lodi was so successful that a second was already being planned. The article, titled "Finished Pleasant Run," observed, "Weather and excellent roads added to the pleasure of the first trip, and aside from broken springs and two or three punctured tires, nothing at all marred the expedition."[117]

The Taylor Inn survived the birth, early childhood and adolescence of the automobile age; eventually, it declined in value and usefulness as a hostel.

After the area's oil drilling boom in 1919 and 1920 provided a bump in profitability, the Taylor Inn transferred ownership and management several times in the 1920s and 1930s. Devoid of use as a hotel in 1937, it briefly avoided sheriff's sale and eventually landed in the hands of the Standard Oil Company. In February 1938, a new Standard Oil Gas Station opened on the site of the Taylor Inn. It prized the location as a new service station rather than a historic structure of a dilapidated luxury hotel. It's ironic to say that it's golden age of prominence was attributable to the automobile, just as its physical death was due to the needs of the automobilist for convenient fuel and service. Its best days served the needs of the motoring public and the people working the oil fields—all tied to the automobile. Its demolition did as well.[118]

Part III

SECOND CENTURY FRAYS

WOMEN'S SUFFRAGE IN MEDINA COUNTY

A Story of Controversy, Uncertainty and Perseverance

*I*n 2020, the nation celebrated one hundred years since women won the right to vote. The events that led up to the historic ratification of the Nineteenth Amendment to the U.S. Constitution were part of the suffrage movement and were filled with controversy and conflict. Many times, the turmoil is overlooked for the final outcome. In 1919, Congress submitted the amendment to the state legislatures, and it was ratified by three-fourths of the states a year later. While the Ohio General Assembly was one of the earliest to ratify, it took until August 1920 and Tennessee's ratification to add the amendment to the U.S. Constitution, effectively giving women full franchise nationwide.

The road to eventual ratification was anything but smooth or short. In Ohio, after passage of a state law in April 1894, women were given the limited right to vote for and serve on school boards. Many who were in favor of the law argued that women would help reform the education system. As Ohio state school commissioner Carson stated, "It is hoped that the women of Ohio will take advantage of the power granted them under the new law and aid in removing from the management of the public schools that narrow partisanship, which, in some localities, is their greatest curse."[119]

On several occasions, even this limited franchise was threatened to be repealed by action of the general assembly, ostensibly because it was not being exercised frequently throughout the state. In fact, Hamilton County officials stated in 1920, out of approximately 50,000 women who were eligible to vote, only 2,000 had been registered to vote under the school franchise and only half of those regularly voted.[120] Sadly, Medina women suffered similarly lackluster involvement at the election day polls. One male observer in the *Medina Sentinel* wrote in a November 1919 election that only 21 women voted in contrast to the 231 men in Ward A of Medina Village. He commented that it was not a very good showing for those who were asking for the franchise to be expanded.

Appearing at the public polling locations on election day was also considered less than proper for some. Many women and men argued across the state that "feminine delicacy" and "refined Christian womanhood" were being injured by women's involvement in the coarseness of politics. As one writer in the *Medina Sentinel* claimed in December 1919, "But let no one forget that the undesirable woman, once with the voting power in her hand, will fully exercise the suffrage given her. The woman who will stay at home will be the honest, conscientious mother with a multitude of duties who feel she is tied down with service."

Unfortunately, despite repeated attempts to broaden the franchise to all elected positions and issues of the state, the women's suffrage movement in Ohio was not fully successful until 1920. Despite the desperate efforts of Ohio suffragists to present their question to the public on its own merits, it was so inextricably drawn into the more bitterly fought "wet" and "dry" contests locally and statewide that it was never possible to overcome the political crosswinds. Typically, "wet" or pro-liquor forces opposed suffrage, while "dry" or temperance passions generally favored the expansion of suffrage.

The political divisiveness was evident throughout the state and in Medina County. Despite the general support of business and community leaders in a few selected communities, a bare majority of Medina County males voted to give full franchise to women in 1912 (51.1 percent)—the measure failed statewide, with only 42.5 percent of men voting in favor. Medina County men defeated it in 1914 and 1919, with only 47.7 percent and 48.3 percent voting "yes." The unremembered discord provides one of the main reasons why celebrations of suffrage by state and local historical societies deserve widespread attention.

All too often, in this age of expected fast-paced changes, we forget the true nature of historical movements. Their outcomes take time, they are not unifying in nature or temperament, and they are not predetermined. There is sometimes a belief that universal franchise was inevitable and widely supported; however, the history and data say otherwise.

TIMELINE OF THE SUFFRAGE STRUGGLE IN MEDINA COUNTY

- April 1894: Ohio law expands suffrage to women over twenty-one years of age to vote for and serve on school boards. Registration to vote was only necessary for those women residing in cities.
- 1912 Special Election for Constitutional Issue No. 23: Statewide, the amendment failed, with only 42.5 percent in favor. It passed countywide with 51.0 percent voting in favor. Leading communities favorable to the full franchise included Sharon (71.0 percent), Granger (68.0 percent), Lodi (67.0 percent) and Westfield (64.0 percent). Opposition was strongest in Liverpool (10.0 percent). Guilford (35.0 percent), Homer (37.0 percent) and Litchfield (37.0 percent).
- 1913 General Election on Constitutional Amendments Proposed by the General Assembly: The eligibility of women to hold appointment as members of boards or positions in departments and institutions affecting or caring for women and children (article XV, section 4) "yes" (435,222) to "no" (225,036)— passed. Medina County 2,376 "yes" to 1,574 "no." Countywide support amounted to 60 percent, with Leroy (Westfield Village), Granger, Sharon and Wadsworth the most in favor, with 77 percent, 74 percent, 72 percent and 69 percent voting "yes," respectively. Montville, Guilford and Liverpool were the least supportive, with only 49 percent, 44 percent and 35 percent voting in favor, respectively.[121]
- 1914: Medina County voters reject women suffrage issue, 2,120 to 2,320. Ohio constitutional amendments proposed by initiative petition to extend the suffrage of women: "yes" 335,390, "no" 518,295—failed with 61 percent voting "no." Countywide, only 48 percent voted in favor, with Sharon (69 percent), Granger (60 percent), Chatham (60 percent) and Lodi Village (58 percent) leading the county. The least supportive communities were Liverpool (14 percent), Guilford (33 percent), Wadsworth Village Ward B (36 percent) and Homer (40 percent).
- 1916: The national Republican and Democratic Party platforms adopted suffrage planks, and the two Ohio party conventions confirmed the national platforms. Supported by these platforms, the legislature of 1917 extended presidential suffrage to Ohio women.

- 1917: Suffrage was again defeated, as the Reynolds Act allowing women to vote for and to be voted for in presidential electors was turned down. Statewide, only 42.6 percent voted in favor. Countywide, the presidential suffrage issue obtained 48 percent of the vote, with Leroy (63 percent), Granger (60 percent), Lodi (56 percent) and Spencer (55 percent) leading. Opposition was strongest in Liverpool (15 percent), Guilford (37 percent), Medina Township (39 percent) and York (39 percent).
- 1919: Presidential suffrage granted by Ohio's Fouts-Reynolds Bill delayed—denied vote in presidential primary of April 27, 1920, when the Ohio Anti-Suffrage Association filed petitions with secretary of state, putting to referendum the Reynolds Presidential Suffrage Bill for the vote in November 1920. Subsequent U.S. Supreme Court ruling nullified the legality of the referendum.[122]
- 1919: Ohio voters in the fall election disapproved legislative ratification of federal constitutional amendments for Prohibition, while another initiative referendum voiding the women's suffrage amendment was pending; the U.S. Supreme Court rules in June 1920 that the ratification of amendments is solely within the power of the general assembly, not the voters of the state. "The method of ratifying amendments, the court held, is a national power specifically granted by the federal constitution and the states have no authority to provide otherwise."[123]
- Congress finally passed the Nineteenth Amendment in 1919. After Congress approved the Nineteenth Amendment, at least thirty-six states needed to vote in favor of it for it to become law. This process is called ratification.
- On June 16, 1919, Ohio voted to ratify the Nineteenth Amendment. In addition, the legislature also passed a bill ensuring Ohio women's right to vote in the upcoming presidential election in November 1920 (in case the amendment was not in effect nationally by then). As it turned out, by August 1920, thirty-six states (including Ohio) had ratified the amendment, and it became part of the U.S. Constitution, ensuring that the right to vote could not be denied on the basis of sex.
- August 18, 1920: The ratification of the Nineteenth Amendment to the U.S. Constitution is completed.

15

CORA M. BLAKESLEE

Successful Medina Merchant and Suffragette

C ora M. (Munson) Blakeslee was described on the celebration of her
ninety-seventh birthday in 1954 as "self-sufficient," a "lover of music"
and "one of Medina's grandest old ladies." She confidently stated at
that time that she never missed an election. The one term not
mentioned in local newspapers accounts over the years, even after her death
in 1956, was *suffragette*, or a political activist. But the evidence suggests, bound
by the convention of civility expected of all proper women in Medina at the
time, that she was both.

She was the daughter of a well-known political figure, Albert Munson,
who served as a civic leader, Republican Party official, state legislator and
probate judge. He also owned the A. Munson & Son hardware store and
served for a time as postmaster in Medina. When Judge Munson died in
1911, his son Lyman briefly ran the hardware store until his death in 1913.
Cora operated the store from then until 1938 with the able assistance of
Walter J. Fenton. The genial and fun-loving Walter "Tim Finnegan" Fenton
was described as her "right arm," and he continued to stay as a manager
with her until the store closed.

She was active in the Republican Party, and upon gaining the full right to
vote in 1920, she frequently served as a precinct election official. Although
the arts, the Medina Library Association, Medina County Historical Society
and "spiritualism" were her passions, she was undoubtedly a political activist
for temperance and suffrage—a frequent combination in Medina County.
She was active in the Woman's Christian Temperance Union, and the local

Cora Munson Blakeslee.
*Courtesy of the Medina
County Historical Society.*

Equal Woman's Suffrage organization listed Cora as a supporter and a hostess of meetings of workers to promote the suffrage ballot issues.[124]

Beyond having Old Glory wave from her homestead flagpole during Republican political campaigns, she took out advertising space in the Democratic Party–leaning newspaper, the *Medina Sentinel*, as well as the Republican-leaning *Medina Gazette*. The advertisements advocated for the suffrage cause under A. Munson & Son in 1912 and 1914. Despite the statewide and countywide losses of the Ohio Constitutional Amendment in 1912, as well as in the 1914 and 1917 referendums, a majority of voters in Medina Village consistently favored the cause. Instead of the regular advertisements promoting stoves, kitchen ware and other hardware, A. Munson & Son used the space to publicly advocate for women's suffrage—something that no other local merchant did. Eventually, the suffrage movement was vindicated with success and a federal constitutional amendment, despite the continued and persistent resistance of the anti-suffrage forces in league with the saloon interests. Although Cora never ran for local office, she was an active voter and staunch Republican who added immeasurably to the political and social life of Medina.

Support for Suffrage Before Business Interests, a Rare Occurrence

Most businesses don't advertise in favor of or in opposition to political issues—and for good reason. Controversial issues can cost businesses their customer support. Consider the suffrage issue in Medina Village in the 1910s. Unlike any other commercial establishment in Medina Village, A. Munson & Son placed advertisements prominently in the local newspapers—Democrat and Republican—urging voters to support the vote for women. D'Armitt's Department Store, M.D. Kimmell Player Pianos, Druggist W.J. Wall, Savings Deposit Bank of Medina, Brainard Jewelry Store, Griesingers' Shoes, Ziegler's Store and Pelton's Grocery & Bakery repetitively placed advertisements mentioning their services and products for women, but none advocated to give women the vote. As shown on the next page, under the ownership of Cora, only A. Munson & Son possessed the fortitude to place an advertisement in favor of the twenty-third amendment to the Ohio Constitution that authorized women's suffrage in both newspapers. Although it passed in Medina

Uncle Biff
TO THE
Voters of Medina County:

Are you going to vote for the Twenty-third Amendment, giving woman the Ballot?

We believe that you are! Because- We believe that the men of Medina County are as just as chivalrous and as far-sighted as the men of any other Country, and can not fail to recognize the fact that woman's aid would be a factor not to be despised in "Governmental Housekeeping."

Because – When such men as Robert M. LaFollette, Theodore Roosevelt, President Thompson of Ohio State University, and large majority of men of their type favor it most earnestly, and women like Jane Adams, Anna Howard Shaw, Prof. Emma Perkins and overwhelming majority of college women are heart and soul in the movement, it proves beyond a doubt that it is a question not to be ignored, or lightly set aside.

Therefore – if you would not put a check upon the spirit of the hour which demands better condition for the greater part of the human race, the spirit which is making for the realization of universal brotherhood vote for the Twenty-third Amendment and see to it, that the great State of Ohio does not lag behind in the march of progress.

A. Munson & Son

Mr. Voter!
Are You Going to Vote for
EQUAL SUFFRAGE?

We believe that you are because we know that the men of Medina county are second to none in intelligence, sagacity and sense of justice.

Woman, through centuries of training, has become an adept in the art of housekeeping, and her aid and counsel in Governmental Housekeeping is a factor not to be despised.

Let Her Help You

Toward the better protection of the home and the maintenance of peace, to the end that our beloved country may never be disgraced by a cruel, beastly, needless war such as is now being waged in Europe.

For only when woman works side by side with man, unfettered in the eyes of the law, can the human race attain its highest development.

"The woman's cause is man's; they rise or sink together, dwarfed or Godlike, bond or free."

A. MUNSON & SON

Left: A facsimile of a Medina advertisement in favor of the twenty-third amendment to the Ohio Constitution, which authorized women's suffrage. *From the* Medina Sentinel, *August 30, 1912.*

Right: A facsimile of an advertisement in the *Medina Gazette* (October 30, 1914), advocating for an amendment to the Ohio Constitution that would expand the vote in all elections to women. *Image created by the author.*

County by a vote of 1,710 to 1,630, it failed statewide, with only 42.5 percent in favor. Sharon Township lead the county, with 71 percent in favor, while Liverpool Township was the least supportive, with only 10 percent in favor.[125]

Two years later, A. Munson & Son was once again the sole business in Medina Village to publicly advocate for suffrage. As noted in an advertisement in the *Medina Sentinel* from October 30, 1914, seen above, Cora Munson advocated for an amendment to the Ohio Constitution that would have expanded the vote in all elections to women. Again, statewide suffrage was defeated by a majority of 144,806 votes. The issue lost in Medina County by 100 votes, despite being passed in all three Medina Village precincts. Countywide, it passed in only fourteen out of the twenty-six precincts.[126]

MYSTERIOUS CIRCUMSTANCES AROUND THE MARRIAGE OF CORA MUNSON THAT REMAIN

*C*ora E. Munson, born in 1857 in River Styx, died at the age of ninety-nine and lived in Medina for seventy-eight years. She was active in business, civic and music affairs throughout her long residence in the village and was well known for her strong beliefs in spiritualism. She married Charles O. Blakeslee, a choir director at St. Paul's Episcopal Church in Medina, when she was forty-three and he was thirty-two. Local accounts said that they left together on a honeymoon and that she returned home alone. According to the reports, he was never seen in Medina again, and Cora only told one other person what happened. Her confidence in a local friend, Mrs. Velma Cochran, was sustained even after her death, as her confidante never publicly disclosed the secret.

Despite obvious suspicions of foul play, Charles O. Blakeslee lived to the age of seventy-eight and thrived in various places, where he became a renowned choir director, organist and "professor" of music. Shortly after his marriage to Cora, they appeared to travel quite a bit from place to place. In 1906, Charles headed a traveling choir based in Lakeside, Ohio, but then contracted a serious illness that then required a time of recuperation at a health resort in Michigan. By 1907, Cora and Charles were reportedly living in Omaha, Nebraska, when her attendance of a family dinner in Seville was mentioned in the *Medina Sentinel* (September 6, 1907), and Charles was hired as a choirmaster and organist at St. James Episcopal Church in Fremont, Nebraska. As mentioned earlier, Cora returned alone to Medina and oversaw the operations of the family business, A. Munson & Son, which her brother Lyman had operated until his death in 1913.

Years later, Charles moved to Butte, Montana, where he taught voice, piano, pipe organ and harmony at the Butte College of Music and Art for nine years. In 1928, he became the permanent organist at Holy Trinity English Lutheran Church in La Crosse, Wisconsin. During that time, he also served as the national president of the Temple of Music Association of America. The last records of his music career placed him in Rockford and Freeport, Illinois, for many years. The notice of his death in 1945 mentions only one immediate family survivor, his sister, Ruth Wittorf, who was living in Butte, Montana—there was no mention of Cora.

There are no records of a divorce filing or a remarriage of either Cora or Charles, and both remained childless. As far as public information reveals, Cora returned to Medina to work and then eventually ran the hardware store, keeping her married name, and she never revealed the circumstances surrounding her physical separation from Charles. Such is the mystery that the *Medina County Gazette* headline explained in 1979: "Many Cora Munson Blakeslee Secrets Will Remain—Secrets."

WOMEN'S SUFFRAGE AND VOTING BY MAIL

Change Is the Law of Life

*I*n 2020, we celebrated the centennial of women winning the right to vote. The events that led up to the historic ratification of the Nineteenth Amendment to the US Constitution was part of the suffrage movement. In 1919, Congress submitted it to the state legislatures, and it was ratified by three-fourths of the states a year later. While the Ohio General Assembly was one of the earliest to ratify, it took until August 1920 and Tennessee's ratification to add the amendment to the U.S. Constitution and effectively give women full franchise nationwide. It is no coincidence that at the same time suffrage was being sought one hundred years ago, there were serious proposals to expand the postal vote to all voters in every election.

SOLDIERS ABSENTEE VOTE CONTROVERSY

Allowing active military members to vote absentee was permitted as long ago as the Civil War for some states, but it was not without controversy. Much is made about the impact of the Union soldier vote in reelecting President Lincoln in 1864. However, many do not realize that for Ohio, the soldier vote was also allowed and influenced the Ohio governor's race of 1863. In addition to Ohio, soldiers from the states of California, Iowa, Maine, Missouri, Pennsylvania and Wisconsin voted in the nonfederal elections that year. In Ohio, the Unionist Party ticket, led by John Brough, was challenged by the Copperhead faction of antiwar Democrats led by

Clement Vallandingham. In Medina County, while Brough received 65 percent of the civilian vote, he obtained 96 percent of the soldier vote.[127]

OHIO 1863 GOVERNOR RACE IN MEDINA COUNTY

Jurisdiction	Brough	%	Vallandingham	%
Brunswick	178	77%	53	23%
Chatham	162	71%	66	29%
Granger	214	88%	30	12%
Guilford	223	62%	138	38%
Harrisville	161	61%	104	39%
Hinckley	220	92%	18	8%
Homer	64	31%	140	69%
Lafayette	181	74%	65	26%
Litchfield	185	84%	35	16%
Liverpool	102	32%	216	68%
Medina	134	78%	37	22%
Medina Village	167	83%	34	17%
Montville	135	67%	67	33%
Sharon	131	49%	134	51%
Spencer	108	53%	95	47%
Wadsworth	192	59%	135	41%
Westfield	136	61%	88	39%
York	140	77%	43	23%
Total	**2,833**	**65%**	**1,498**	**35%**
soldier vote	323	96%	14	4%
Total	**3,156**	**68%**	**1,512**	**32%**

Source: A. Severence. "Common Pleas Clerk's Office." *Medina County Gazette*, November 17, 1863.

But the political party labels were not as fixed as one might think. The soldiers' vote issue was also controversial in almost every state of the Union. The wartime battlefield was replicated in the political battlefield—everything was about the Civil War and the causes for the disunion. During the Civil War, in 1863, the "Union Party" in Ohio was formed by a temporary fusion of Republican Party, former Whig Party members and the prowar Democrats, poised against the antiwar Democrats, or so-called Copperheads. Each group had their respective state conventions, but they were not held under the guise of the Republican or Democratic Parties. Instead, they were the Union State Ticket versus the Democratic Union Ticket in a true test over the state participation—money and manpower—in a civil war in which many communities were likewise divided.[128]

For the Union State ticket, the Union Republican Convention was held in Columbus on June 17, 1863. After a series of votes for each office, the convention nominated former Democrat John Bough for governor, followed by Republican Colonel Charles Anderson for lieutenant governor, Republican Colonel James H. Godman was the nominee for state auditor and the candidate for treasurer of state was incumbent and former Democrat G. Volney Dorsey.[129]

The Democratic Union ticket was full of Democrats—Clement L. Vallandigham for governor, George E. Pugh for lieutenant governor, William Hubbard for auditor of state and Horace S. Knapp for treasurer of state. Pugh was a very strong statewide candidate on his own, having been a former member of the Ohio House of Representatives, a state attorney general from 1852 to 1854 and United States senator for a single term, from 1855 to 1861. Hubbard and Knapp were both editors and journalists of Copperhead Democratic newspapers. Pugh, Hubbard and Knapp all received more votes in the 1863 election than the head of the ticket, Vallandigham—probably owing to his notable forced exile to Canada by the Union, as well as his ardent and fiery anti-Union rhetoric and rebellious personality. The convention that nominated them all ran on the Democratic Union ticket, but of course, they were materially supported by the Democratic political machine.[130]

One decisive and controversial issue in the election was the absentee soldier vote. As you can imagine, Democrats argued against it, while Unionists felt a more lenient approach was warranted, given the stakes and the circumstances. An attempt to give the absentee soldiers a vote was made in the general assembly on a bill that was introduced on February 28, 1862. It was held up in a house committee until two days before the scheduled adjournment of the session—barely enough time to process in the other chamber. The general consensus was to consider it in the next session, once the political ramifications for each respective side had been considered.

Reportedly, in the 1863 session, the Copperhead Democrats tried to attach a "poison" amendment to the proposal that would have created a conflict between the house and senate versions of the bill; it was hoped that these irreconcilable differences would effectively stall the bill. The Democrats had to be very careful when challenging the bill so that they didn't appear to be undermining the legitimate rights of these volunteer soldiers and unappreciative of their service. Of course, the debate centered around concerns of fraud, coercion, perjury and transparency.

At first, the legal challenge went all the way to the Ohio Supreme Court on a technical issue of whether the general assembly had the authority to devise an election process outside the legal boundaries of the State of Ohio. Arguably, the system of selecting election judges, casting votes, creating poll books all outside of the normal boundaries of local election officials was a new concept. The Copperheads argued that the general assembly could only create a system within the state for soldiers who were physically voting in the state. The Ohio Supreme Court rejected the challenges and upheld the constitutionality of the bill. The election of 1863 continued in all its contentious splendor and rancor.[131]

The debate in favor of the soldier votes often adopted the following points, as articulated by a soldier writing from his post in Virginia and serving in the 166th Ohio Volunteer Infantry (OVI):

> *The truth is, the soldiers have as much, yes more, interest in the domestic and political affairs of our country than they ever had. The Ohio soldier is deeply interested in Ohio; and why should he not be? His home is there; his property is there; his family is there; he pays taxes there; and would be there himself, did not a higher duty than self-interest call him hence.*[132]

The Democrats, genuinely concerned about the political effect of the votes on their ticket, argued that the military officers purposefully and systematically hindered communications back home, especially those involving political matters. As one soldier reported in the *Cincinnati Enquirer*:

> *The private soldier desires peace, and the attempts that have been made by certain of their officers and by abolition presses at home to make it appear otherwise is an imposition and is so regarded by the soldiers. The fact that their superior officers permit only a certain class of papers to be read by the soldiers increases the indignation they feel at the attempts made to misrepresent their viewpoints.*[133]

Another point of concern was the effect of conducting elections in the middle of a military camp in which the soldiers' voting preferences would likely be known. Soldiers, upon requesting a ballot, asked for tickets listing all of the candidates of their preferred party. The "secret ballot" process that we know today was not in use then, and the initial tallies were not necessarily secret to the officers overseeing the elections either. This point is especially troublesome when viewing a public newspaper account of the votes cast by Ohio volunteer army units stationed in Maryland. "On two tickets, Brough's name was erased from personal objections and no other substituted. The name of the soldier so recreant to duty as to vote for a traitor is pretty well ascertained to be a certain Patrick Laughlin of the 55th OVI and formerly known as a hard shell Democrat."[134]

More to the point, Democrats accused officers of coercion:

> *We have repeatedly alluded to the farce of having elections held in our military camps, where the soldiers are coerced by their officers either to vote as they may indicate or to stay from the polls altogether. It is an outrage on the sanctity of the ballot box, and the vote taken is no index of the feelings of the soldiers. It only shows the views of the officers, and too many of them, having an eye to promotion, seek to curry favor by absolutely compelling the men to vote in such way as the administration may dictate.*[135]

A soldier from the First Brigade, Gordan's Division, wrote to the editor of the *Wayne County Democrat* about how the officers brought in Union Party stump speakers, followed by threats of punishment for voting for the Democrat ticket, and they were given duty assignments that prevented them from voting at assigned times and places. Lastly, as the soldier reported, "They opened a secret poll at the commissary and got all of the Brough men to vote that were present. In the evening, it leaked out and some Democrats went to vote. Two of three got their votes in, but as soon as the abolitionists saw that the Democrats had found out the secret and were coming to vote, they closed the polls before the time provided by law. We were fairly cheated out of our votes by our own officers."[136]

After the results started to come in from afield, of course the Democrats pressed on their public objections of fraud and perjury. As the *Cincinnati Enquirer* editorial offered:

> *The "soldier vote" in Ohio, as the practice is facetiously called, of the administration using the army to subserve its party purposes will, it is*

thought, reach 42,000, about all of which was cast for Brough. There must be at least 65,000 votes in the army from Ohio, so about one third of the soldiers entitled to vote did not do so, probably because they could not conscientiously, without embroiling themselves with their employers and paymasters at Washington in a difficulty in which they would suffer.[137]

Accusations of voter fraud targeted local elections officials who were tasked with canvassing the soldiers votes and including them in the election totals.[138] Brough and the entire Union ticket were eventually declared the legal winners of the contests, including the contentious soldiers' votes. Brough's majority on the home front vote was 61,703, and on the soldiers' vote, it was 39,179—in all, his majority totaled 100,882 votes. Vallandigham carried thirty-two of the eighty-eight counties on the home vote but only seventeen on the combined vote. Even without the soldier vote, Brough and the state ticket won. The same could not necessarily be said for some of the local races.

The statewide victory prompted President Abraham Lincoln to wire Brough, "Glory to God in the highest. Ohio has saved the nation." Notably, the soldier vote was less critical for the ultimate victory of the pro-Union forces in the 1863 election than in the outcome of the presidential contest in 1864. Regardless, it demonstrated that even during a Civil War, elections could be conducted with absentee votes; however, it was not done without considerable political and legal controversy.[139]

More Changes and More Controversy

During the suffrage movement, there was also a parallel push to provide increased voter access to the polls, especially for men with occupations that involved a lot of traveling via along the nation's extensive railroad networks. An editorial in the Coshocton newspaper the *Tribune* argued, "For years, it was the custom of the party to pay the way of the voter back to his hometown in order that he vote 'right.' The harm of thus placing men under obligation to some party or faction or candidate is too apparent to merit discussion. In too many instances, the voter, in thus accepting car fare, was morally guilty of accepting a bribe, for he generally voted for that party of candidate who 'paid the most for his railroad ticket.'"[140]

Voting by mail became an often-heard suggestion, and in some regards, it was an enhancement to the suffrage vote. As I mentioned in an earlier chapter, many argued that "feminine delicacy" and "refined Christian womanhood" might be injured by women's involvement in the coarseness of politics and their forced visits to undesirable polling locations, should they be given the vote. Voting by mail was presented as an opportunity to protect the proper woman from those morally threatening circumstances.

The *Medina Sentinel* argued in December 1919 that voting by mail should be tried for convenience and, if no other reason, that it would save women voters from both insult and jostling at polls or "button-holing" on the streets. In addition, the author argued that voting by mail lessoned the influences of the big city political machines, greatly reduced election day costs and poll worker time and eliminated "many evils, the canvassing board having ample time to run down all irregularities or suspicious conditions."[141]

Nationally, both political parties throughout the country advocated for voting by mail in the first two decades of the twentieth century. Ohio Republican governor Frank B. Willis, in his inaugural message to the Republican-dominated Eighty-First General Assembly in January 1915, urged legislation that would create a system for registering and voting by mail. World War I started a mere five months after this proposal was introduced by the governor, so other economic and war preparation issues took precedent for a while. In 1920, Ohio finally enacted some provisions for absentee voting, which required a notarized application.[142]

Even American presidents started to avail themselves of voting absentee, starting with President Woodrow Wilson and his wife in 1920. In 1924, it was noted that President Calvin Coolidge wanted to economize by voting by mail. "The president, it was said today, believes that the present is a good time to set an example of thrift. At a time when he is urging different government departments to cut down expenses, he believes he hardly is warranted in spending money that a trip to Northampton would entail."[143] By 1924, Ohio would be among the twenty-six states that would grant voting by mail in all elections to qualified voters who were temporarily absent from their homes on election day. This is not quite the universal voting-by-mail proposal that Governor Willis envisioned or the one that the progressive wing of the Republican Party and Democratic Party officials suggested nationally, but it was a start.[144]

President John F. Kennedy once said, "Change is the law of life. And those who look only to the past or present are certain to miss the future." Consider the explanation offered by prominent columnist and minister Dr. Frank Crane when he observed in 1919:

Why has not voting by mail been adopted long ago? Simply because we are dominated by ghosts, not reason. That is why the English still use their absurd pounds, shillings, and pence, men keep on using six-button suspenders instead of two-button, all table d'hôtel dinners run the same course from soup to coffee, and the U.S. Senate continues to play party politics while the world is on fire.[145]

I would agree that change is the law of life, and quite often, our ghosts still appear to dominate our reason, even as the U.S. Senate continues to play party politics. Thank goodness for the demise of six-button suspenders!

18

CELEBRATING THE END OF WORLD WAR I

Once Was Not Enough

The end of World War I and the announcement of an armistice with Germany brought great celebration to Medina in early November 1918. The armistice was to end fighting on land, sea and air in World War I between the Allies and their opponents, including Germany. For Medina Village, it apparently brought two celebrations.

The *Medina Sentinel* reported on November 8, 1918, headlines that read, "Heard War Was Over: Citizens Uproarious." Further reporting, "Bedlam broke loose in Medina at 2 o'clock Thursday afternoon when word came from Cleveland that Germany had accepted unconditionally the terms for an armistice offered to her, and for two hours, bells were rung, whistles blown, guns exploded and men, women and children yelled themselves hoarse in jubilation. Local speakers addressed the crowd from the band stand. Flags were hoisted from the business houses." Unavoidably, the so-called bedlam had to quickly cease when another bulletin was received shortly thereafter stating that the first one was in error. A rumor printed as fact by the *Cleveland Press* led many in Medina Village to prematurely celebrate. The Germans had only been handed the armistice terms—they had not actually signed it yet.

Perhaps we can't blame the Medina people for being a little cautious before another "spontaneous" celebration could occur the following Monday, November 11, at noon. In what the *Akron Beacon Journal* headline for the day proclaimed, "Armistice Reduces Foe to Absolute Impotence," communities throughout the land held peace parades, impromptu concerts by community bands and organized programs with speeches by politicians, clergymen and prominent businessmen, all celebrating the conclusion of the war in Europe.

Medina again, in the words of the *Medina Sentinel* headline, observed righteous celebration: "Pandemonium as Pageant in Medina Signalizes End of War." According to the front-page report, Medina people, "at the dawn of Monday, began to evacuate all the pent-up anxiety of the past four years to make room for an eighteen-hour feast of unadulterated fun."

So, what did pandemonium and unadulterated fun look like in the little village of Medina a century ago? Apparently, it included a peace parade organized by the mayor, concerts by Seville and Medina community bands, an exhibition by the Ingham martial band and organized programs with speeches by politicians, clergymen and prominent businessmen all celebrating the conclusion of the war. The celebration reportedly brought thousands of young and old people from all over the county to the village. However, the newspaper was good enough at the end of the story to make note that there was very little evidence of intoxication.

I would hope so, given that just the week before in the general election, 66 percent of the Medina Village voters had approved a statewide prohibition on all intoxicating beverages. This two-to-one victory in the battle against alcohol was well above the 51 percent who approved of it statewide. After all, sobriety in Medina Village was still important, even amid pandemonium and unadulterated fun.

19

THE MEDINA TIME CONUNDRUM OF 1919

Does Anybody Really Know What Time It Is?

*T*he rock band Chicago's refrain "Does anybody really know what time it is?" went through my head as I read a *Medina Sentinel* headline from December 27, 1918: "Time Conundrum for Medina People." The article explained a dilemma for Medina County a century ago, in which they were in the middle of a decades-long dispute between federal, state and local governments over who would determine the official time.

Prior to the advent of a nationwide network of railroads, timekeeping was largely a local decision. As railroads swept across the country and schedules had to be coordinated, the need for standard time zones became obvious. In 1893, the Ohio General Assembly established Central Standard Time as the official time throughout the state. Although it had been used on all Ohio railroads for some years before, varying local customs and preferences had prevailed. The law set a new standard for all public offices, banks and courts. Even then, large portions of Ohio remained adherent to the Eastern Standard Time Zone, resulting in a zigzag pattern between the two time zones across Ohio.

In Medina County, the keepers of the official public time were the county commissioners, through their possession and control of the courthouse clock tower. That meant Central Standard Time (CST) was used for all official county and legal events. For some, however, like the interurban Cleveland Southwestern & Columbus Railway—which ran north–south through the county, connecting Cleveland to Wooster, Ashland and Mansfield—the Eastern Standard Time (EST) was specified for its timetable until 1915.

Medina Village was also divided timewise for a while. For example, the October 1915 issues of the *Medina Sentinel* had postings of Sipher's Grocery, Warner-Hemmeter Company Store and the Medina Woman's Christian Temperance Union with published EST schedules. The Congregational church and the Methodist Episcopal church also used EST for their scheduled services in the first part of 1915, but by mid-October, they started to publish times in CST. By 1918, CST was apparently winning over EST for most events in Medina County. Nonetheless, the growing consensus for CST ended with World War I.

In 1919, the Interstate Commerce Commission, empowered by the 1918 Standard Time Act, ordered Ohio into the Eastern Time Zone. In the same legislation, the Daylight Saving Time (DST) order further complicated the time issue. Daylight Saving Time (DST) was extremely unpopular, and the intended savings in energy and increased productivity were, at the best, arguable, if not speculative. Congress eventually repealed the section concerning daylight saving time later in 1919—over President Woodrow Wilson's veto. Afterward, DST became a local option until World War II.

So, what was the conundrum for Medina in early 1919? The clocks first had to be set ahead one hour to adjust from Central to Eastern Standard Time in January, and then they had to be adjusted another full hour ahead in April to comply with the DST order from the federal government. So, from December 31, 1918, to April 1, 1919, Medina County people were asked to jump ahead two full hours in a matter of three months. In true Medina fashion, the village, as well as the county commissioners, refused to adopt the DST plan and kept the courthouse clock and village times set to EST. As the *Medina Sentinel* observed, "Sun time is one and half hours slower than the new federal time, which shows how much clocks are put out of kilter in this section under the daylight saving law." Given that there were no federal penalties for ignoring the DST law, Medina County officials risked little by respecting local wishes and common sense.

Daylight Saving Time remains a somewhat controversial issue today, a century later. Only two states and four U.S. territories do not observe it— Hawaii, Arizona, American Samoa, Guam, Puerto Rico and the Virgin Islands. Under current federal law, states can opt out of DST, which requires the spring and fall time changes. However, in 2021, twenty-eight states are considering legislation to adopt "permanent daylight saving time" (staying on summer hours all year with no time shifts), which requires congressional action to take effect.

A 1905 postcard depicting the Medina County Courthouse. *Author's collection.*

When I was a state legislator, I received perennial phone calls to my office that were critical of the time changes and asked for reconsideration on Ohio's participation. In 2020, the Ohio General Assembly enacted a resolution encouraging Congress to allow groups of states to adopt permanent DST. A thoughtful review and study of the purported benefits and consequences of DST in America's vibrant 24/7 economy is probably overdue. In the meantime, we can all rejoice that the central timepiece of our county in 1919—the Medina County Courthouse Clock—is still ticking in 2021. In the age of digital watches, it is nice to live in a community that appreciates preserving that part of our history, even though it is no longer the official keeper of public time.

20

PICK A SIDE ALREADY

Opportunities for Political Bridge Building Lost

I n 1922, the office for Medina County surveyor was up for election, and the Republican and Democratic Parties initially nominated the same person: Fremont E. Tanner. Tanner, born in Chatham, graduated from Sharon High School, earned a college education in Valaparasio, Indiana, and at Ohio Northern University. He entered the engineering trade with practical experiences building roads and bridges and supervising the tax drafting department for the Summit County engineer. He then became the village engineer in Hardin, Montana, and built thirty-six miles of track from the Big Horn Canyon to Custer, Montana, on the Northern Pacific Railroad. He returned to the area and after working as a village engineer and commercial surveyor; then he decided to run for Medina County surveyor.[146]

That county position, a precursor to the county engineer, was an elective office for a three-year term starting in 1831. According to the Medina County highway engineer's office, by the end of the nineteenth century, the county surveyor was almost totally involved in building and maintaining roads, bridges and drainage ditches. In 1915, the Ohio General Assembly established a salary for the office and gave them the responsibility of also being a resident engineer for the state highway department.

The simultaneous nomination of Tanner for county surveyor happened almost by accident—it was not the intent of either party's leadership. He actively campaigned in both the local Republican and Democratic newspapers at the time—the *Medina Gazette* and the *Medina Sentinel*—from the fall of 1921 to August 8, 1922, the date of the respective party primary elections. On the Republican primary ballot, the votes for the three candidates resulted in the following totals: Fremont E. Tanner, 1,553; Walter R. Bibbins, 1,185; and Claud C. Crawford, 977. Tanner won the Republican Party nomination handily.[147]

When the Democrats had filled out their county tickets several weeks prior, no one had stepped forward, and on primary election day, two write-in candidates emerged: Fremont E. Tanner and Ivan R. Ault. Tanner received more votes than Ault in the Democratic primary, solely from the write-ins. Democratic Party leadership swiftly contended that Tanner could only run for the office on one party ticket and declared for Ault. Ault was already a deputy surveyor for the incumbent surveyor, Walter R. Bibbins, who had just lost the Republican nomination to retain the office to Tanner. He was qualified and experienced, there is no doubt, but Tanner had a different opinion.

Fremont E. Tanner, along with Republican Party leadership, argued that he had won both primaries fair and square. Ohio secretary of state Harvey C. Smith, a Republican, ruled on August 18 that under primary election laws, a Republican could not legally be nominated on a Democratic Party ballot. Irvin R. Ault would be the Democratic Party candidate, and Fremont E. Tanner would be the Republican Party candidate for Medina County surveyor, to be elected on November 7, 1922. Tanner had easily beaten the Republican incumbent surveyor, Bibbins, and was destined to win against Ault. Within two months—eight months earlier than scheduled—he was appointed to the unexpired term of office by county commissioners following the death of the County Surveyor Bibbins. Before he was appointed, Tanner had to pledge to the board of commissioners that he would retain the office staff, which included his former Democratic rival, Ault.[148]

Fremont E. Turner would only serve one term as Medina County surveyor. He was badly defeated for renomination by one of his deputy surveyors, W.W. Anderson, and the Republican Party voters in the August primary in 1924. It was a very rocky term of office for Tanner. Early on, he complained that his predecessor had expended two years in advance all of the constructions funds that were needed for improvements beyond maintenance. Apparently, he also lost some assigned road work from the state transportation department, which typically provided additional money to the county coffers. He was in only his fourth month as county surveyor when the board accused him of making false statements against the commissioners in the *Medina Gazette* and *Medina Sentinel*. According to the commissioners' journal, the county prosecutor was brought in to validate the board's claims and found in their favor. The board, after demanding and failing to get a retraction from Tanner, unanimously adopted a formal resolution declaring the surveyor guilty of misconduct in office and grossly neglecting his duties. They requested his resignation from the office of surveyor. Unyielding, Tanner refused to resign or retract his assertions, and despite the best efforts of County Prosecutor Weber, he maintained his independence from the board's meddling.[149]

The board of county commissioners adopted an attitude of fiscal austerity. They formally rejected the funding for Tanner's county road program on May 19, 1924. This back and forth over projects and funding would eventually lead to a lawsuit for funding against the county commissioners. Tanner was criticized several times by the county commissioners for not following lawful orders to draw up plans, estimates and specifications for some county roadways. Tanner even took an argument against the commissioners to the state attorney general over who the legal custodian of county property was—it was the commissioners, according to the state. To complicate political matters further, in the summer of 1924, criminal assault charges were lodged against him by *Medina Gazette* editor W.B. Baldwin, a staunch and respected Republican who had publicly criticized his work.[150]

There was an uncomfortably long period of time between Tanner's Republican primary defeat on August 8, 1924, and his last day in office as the surveyor, September 6, 1925. Between criminal proceedings and civil lawsuits over funding, Tanner eventually worked out an agreement with County Prosecuting Attorney Seymour to drop the criminal cases against him. He left town for good and deposited his check of $18.70 for court costs with the county clerk of courts. Eventually, he found his way back out west, working in the engineering department of the AC&Y Railroad; he also served as a municipal engineer. He passed away at the age of sixty-eight in Oxford, Nebraska, in 1954.[151]

Imagine how things might have been different if Tanner had been permitted to appear on both the Democrat and Republican Party ballots in 1922. For those knowledgeable of the history of American politics, this is not as farfetched an idea as many would currently think. Presidential election history has, on one occasion, seen a national candidate appear on the general election ballots representing different parties. William Jennings Bryan was endorsed in the 1896 presidential campaign by the Democratic Party, Populist Party and the National Silver Party. All three party ballots had different vice presidential running mates.

Changes of state law since the 1912 Ohio Constitutional Convention have solidified the control of the two major parties over the mechanisms of election. They have more or less guaranteed that party nominations through election primaries translate into victories for their respective party, thereby diminishing the chances of third or minor parties nominating and electing entire slates of candidates for offices. Occasionally, one independent or third-party candidate might be elected at a local, county or even legislative district level, but never would anyone think that a single person could be so strongly supported across political party boundaries that they could appear on a ballot representing both parties.

Some could argue that the divide between parties is so immutable that a single candidate could not ever "bridge" the differences between them. While Tanner's apparent battles with a bipartisan board of commissioners and others is clear evidence that he was never actually in danger of becoming that political bridge builder. Moreover, it is still intriguing to think, what if the law allowed such a possibility? Maybe the seemingly unending and often unproductive battle between parties could be better managed if, on occasion, we allowed both parties to nominate the best person for an elected job—especially one that is more technical than political, like that of a county engineer or a coroner—and build a few more political bridges than political walls.

Part IV

THE MIXED BLESSINGS OF SWIFT CHANGES

FIXING STATE ROUTE 18 "SUICIDE ROAD" TOOK A BIT LONG TO COMPLETE

*H*istorically, the east–west road passing through Medina has always been a major connector of our county seat to northeast and northwestern Ohio. The road was somewhat improved for the War of 1812 to assist the movement of the militia westward to meet the challenges of the British occupation of Detroit and to oppose threats from the Natives of northwest Ohio to patriotic settlements.

Named after pioneer Martin Smith of Portage County, it was the first road established in that area in 1809 and was recut from Old Portage westward by the Fourth Division of the Ohio Militia, under Major General Elijah Wadsworth. According to reports, hundreds of teams loaded with supplies, provisions, ammunitions and troops traversed the road to Camp Avery in Milan. Between September 1812 and February 1813, this fortified encampment defended the Western Reserve from Native attacks and a possible British invasion of northern Ohio. General Simon Perkins, while commanding the Third Brigade of the Fourth Division, likewise used Smith Road in his journey to reach Fort Stephenson in Fremont in 1813.[152]

While most of it was originally named Smith Road, eventually, the length of the road in Medina County was called Medina Road to the east and Norwalk Road to west. In the 1920s, it received the designation as a state route, SR-95 from Medina Village eastward and SR-291 westward from the village, and then, in 1923, it was given the number 18 for the entire length through the county. While the responsibility for this essential highway to the Medina County seat came under the state highway department, sufficient funding for improvements, the removal of dangerous sections and even covering annual maintenance costs were always a challenge.

In the 1920s, Ohio government officials, businesses and citizens were struggling with how best to fund state roads that were driven on by the rising tide of the automobiles. The fairest or most expedient manner to fund state highways was certainly in the eye of the beholder—or rather the user and beneficiary. In the nineteenth century, public roadway conditions were the yearly responsibility of the property owner because they benefitted directly.

Similarly, the debate over distributing the costs of completing the vision of the "good roads movement," largely led by farmers and merchants, met active resistance among many property owners and taxpayers. The political question divided many, so any resolution came painfully. Transportation historian H. Roger Grant summarized Ohio's approach to highway funding after the first several decades of the automobile era: "Since the state embraced a pay-as-you-go approach, relying heavily on modest gasoline and motor vehicle taxes, revenues never generated the money needed to modernize the state system of approximately sixteen thousand miles of surfaced roads."[153]

The main highway for Medina County that attracted federal and state attention was the Wooster Pike, which connected Cleveland to Wooster and a connecting point to the transcontinental U.S.-30 or Lincoln Highway. In an age of "pay as you go" highway funding and the general experiences of scarcity during the Depression era, Route 18 took a back seat in priority for state and federal funding. For years, due to the rough brick pavement, lack of proper width and numerous accidents along the stretch between Medina and Montrose, it was called "death road." It served more than five thousand vehicles a day by 1939.[154] It became an important route for commercial and industrial traffic, particularly the stretches of highway between Akron and Norwalk. It was said to be "the most heavily traveled truck road in Ohio, accommodating movement of trucks from rubber manufacturers in Akron to Detroit automobile center, and also from the steel center at Canton and Massillon to Detroit."[155]

A Route 18 Association was formed with chapters among the villages along the route in the late 1930s. The group provided advertising literature that claimed Route 18 was the shortest route between Chicago and New York City and thereby was deserving of more state funding.[156] Among the many improvements that the Route 18 Association pushed for was the construction of eight and a half miles of twenty-two-foot-wide concrete pavement westbound along the existing eighteen-foot-wide pavement. It was

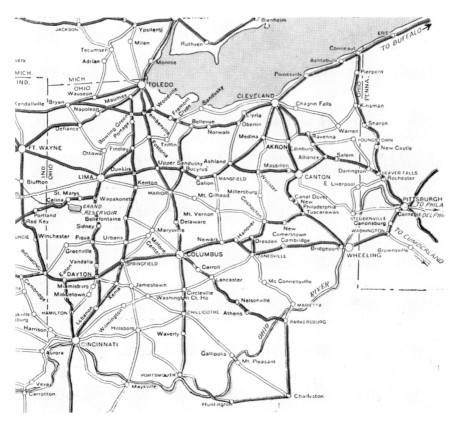

Major highway maps published in 1915 included the future U.S.-42, SR-3 and SR-18 as main routes through Medina County to adjoining counties. *A scanned portion of "Gulf Refining Company Road Map of Middle West States," in* The Official Automobile AAA Blue Book: A Touring Hand-Book of the Principal Automobile Routes in the Central States, 15th Year *(Chicago: Automobile Blue Book Publishing Company, 1915).*

to be a divided highway at first, thereby allowing the existing traffic to move while the new section was being constructed. Because the new construction followed modern engineering standards, which limited the steepness of hills that loaded trucks had to convey, many hills were eliminated. Many of the eastbound Route 18 hills and dips remained in the repaving of the roadway. At the time, some expressed hope that future state projects would complete that section as well. But who knew then those frequent users of Route 18 would suffer a bifurcated grade for over sixty years?

The time came for celebration when the westbound part of the roadway was completed in late 1941. Newly elected Medina County prosecutor William Batchelder Jr. served as banquet toastmaster at a celebration of the

133

Before and after (1938 versus 1941) pictures of SR-18. These photographs show the new asphalt pavement and bifurcated, divided roadways that would remain for sixty years. *Courtesy of the Medina County Historical Society.*

Route 18 Association on Friday, December 4, 1941, at the Mayflower Hotel, the junction of Routes 18 and 176, in Akron. Highway engineers from Medina and Summit Counties, as well as 150 officials and highway boosters, collectively celebrated the formal opening of the new Medina Road.[157]

According to the *Medina County Gazette*, Prosecutor Batchelder served as the substitute toastmaster of the event—prominent Medina attorney James B. Palmquist was originally scheduled but was unable to attend. Nancy Spitzer of Medina and Don Mell Jr. of Fairlawn, ten-year old youths, were selected to cut the blue-and-white ribbon stretched across the road at the opening ceremony. The East High School band of Akron furnished music for the event organized by the Akron Chamber of Commerce.[158]

The principal speaker at the banquet was the Ohio State highway superintendent Hal Sours. He stated that major improvements in highway construction had to be confined to roads designated for defense use. However, he also suggested "now was the time to draw up a well-formed program of highway improvement to take up unemployment at the end of the war. A well-defined program now to be in readiness when employment in the future becomes slack would eliminate the waste of a hastily wrought program."[159]

The war effort Superintendent Sours spoke about on December 4 did not involve the United States in the same way that it would following the surprise Japanese attack on Pearl Harbor on December 7, 1941. It was not only a day that would live in infamy, but it was also a day that changed the world, the lives of millions and the priorities of state transportation funding. That section of State Route 18 wouldn't successfully be revisited, reengineered or constructed for sixty years.

The dedication of the new million-dollar "model highway" between Medina and Akron was celebrated by both counties. The divided highway and the elimination of curves and hills reduced driving hazards to a minimum. The Medina County portion of the project cost $750,000. Locals boasted of the improvement: "Once known to truckers as 'suicide road,' this 20-mile stretch of Route 18 is now one of the best in the state and will be one of the best in the nation when the south strip in Medina County is repaved."[160]

Superintendent Sours assured, "Regarding the south lane of Route 18 in Medina County, the highway director (Hal Sours) said it was wearing out faster than expected.…He said there was no immediate plan to improve the lane to match the improved north lane; however, he said he believed it would be soon."[161] While the attack on Pearl Harbor and the demands of World War II may have interrupted plans to reconstruct the south lane, there is little doubt that the demand for such improvements increased dramatically. By 2000, county officials argued before a state board, empowered to prioritize highway projects called Transportation Review Advisory Council (TRAC), that they should fund the project because it was long overdue. Officials reminded them that World War II was over, the Korean War was over, the Vietnam War was over and even the Cold War was over. At the start of a new century, they pleaded with Ohio Department of Transportation (ODOT) to make the commitment to finally finish the project—even if it was sixty years later than originally hoped.

Increased traffic, up to twenty-four thousand vehicles a day; numerous accidents; and persistence paid off. Identified as a major ODOT project, State Route 18 was reconstructed from Windfall Road to the Summit County line starting in 2004, and it was completed in 2007. The total cost was $19.4 million and was divided as follows: $2 million in local contributions, $1.8 million from ODOT District 3, $1.6 million from a demonstration grant program and $14.0 million from TRAC funding.[162]

There was a grand ribbon-cutting in 2006 to celebrate the project. In attendance was the former Medina County prosecutor William G. Batchelder Jr., the father of future speaker of the Ohio House William G. Batchelder III, who served as toastmaster of the celebration on December 4, 1941. He was ninety-two at the time. In an interview with the *Akron Beacon Journal* in 2006, he observed about the project, "It's pretty late in the game if you ask me," he said, chuckling. "But this is typical of politics—it's red hot today, deader than a door nail the next."[163]

In a private interview with me at the time, the head of the Batchelder clan confided that, although he was greatly honored to be part of the celebration in 2006, he actually didn't recall being toastmaster of the first opening on 1941. I expressed to him that it was entirely understandable, given the number of years between the two. And shortly after the first event, he volunteered and joined the U.S. Army in the war effort, which must have created a whole host of new memories as he served his country. I commented at the time that it had to be true; after all, it was in all of the newspapers. We both chuckled at that one as well.

1939

"Fuedin Farmers" in Brunswick Drew Nationwide Attention and Statewide Reform

Billboards welcoming people to Medina County have not typically included a coverall-clad shotgun-toting sentry. Just as rare is someone guarding a thirty-two-foot-by-eight-foot illuminated sign warning visitors that they were entering the "home of the garbage-fed hog, the garbage dumping ground for Cuyahoga County." The sign was erected on a one-hundred-acre property along U.S.-42 in Brunswick Township in mid-January 1939. It belonged to the vice-president of a Cleveland hardware firm who was described by his rural neighbors as a "gentlemen" farmer, Elmer Eyssen. Yes, it was the future site of Medina County's no. 1 tourist attraction, Mapleside Farms.

The unique signage had the support of many residents who neighbored the 250-acre hog farm that were offended by the foul smells of the 1,500 hogs being supplied with thirty tons of garbage daily from Cleveland and Cleveland Heights starting in 1938. The Medina health commissioner and a majority of the health district board had originally sided with the farmer. "Pigs is pigs, and this country around here is strictly farmland," explained hog farmer Frank H. Harper. Originally dismissing the complaints, the inaction prompted the billboard, armed guard, public embarrassment and nationwide attention. The *Medina Gazette* publicly counseled Eyssen to correct the problem by other means, commenting, "It casts an improper reflection on the whole county of Medina. The wording on it has not added to your prestige."

Within the month of the billboard and nationwide press, the Ohio Public Health Council, following a Columbus hearing from the opposing parties, ordered the health district to decide one way or another if the hog farm was operating as a public nuisance. Although R.E. Snedden, a Medina County prosecutor, had advised the Medina board that they were not legally required to make a decision, the council threatened state action. On March 31, the health board, with the support of their health commissioner Dr. Irvin B. Kievit, ruled 3–2 that it was not a public nuisance. Kievit stated that the repulsive odor of the hog farm "could not be declared a health menace or factories, manufacturing rubber goods, chemicals and other commodities would come under the same classification."[164]

In the meantime, the statewide debate over municipal garbage and hog farms took an added vigor throughout northeast Ohio. East Liberty, Green and Springfield communities in Summit County similarly fought against Akron City garbage going to the Ohio Stock Food Company hog farms in those areas. An injunction was then filed in the Medina case to stop the hauling and large-scale dumping of the city garbage. Cuyahoga County Common Pleas and District Appeals Courts sided with residents long enough for the public to prevail on the health board to reconsider the ruling. Eventually, the injunction made it to the Ohio Supreme Court, but by then, the issue was settled in Medina County.

With the entrance of new member, Dr. R.L. Mansell from Wadsworth, and a reversal in the position of the Seville Village representative Roy Chambers, the Medina County Health Board revisited the issue. On June 6, the health board reversed itself with a vote of 4–1, declaring that the garbage-fed pig farm was a public nuisance and that Harper had ninety days to abate the problem. They also accepted the resignation of Commissioner Kievit, following a public request to tender one because of "gross neglect of duty."[165]

In the first half of the twentieth century, the garbage coming out of Ohio's cities was mostly food waste. Glass and metals were too precious to dispose of and were well worth their manual removal for reuse or recycling. Modern plastics were nonexistent. Farmers, cities and public health officials were in the middle of a battle over problems with garbage-fed livestock. Most major cities since the 1910s and 1920s had established relationships with country farms for the regular disposal of their garbage. Public health professionals nationwide, however, had come across substantial evidence that without tight controls over the raw garbage, human trichinosis and the spread of endemic typhus and plague would likely result. The U.S.

RISE OF PROMINENT POLITICAL FAMILY TIED TO BRUNSWICK PIG FARM CONTROVERSY

The rise of one of the most politically prominent families in Ohio, the Batchelder clan, owes much to this dispute between a pig farmer and the owners of Mapleside Farms. R.E. Snedden, the Medina County prosecutor at the time, sided with pig farmer Frank H. Harper, which ended up being a rather unpopular position, especially in Brunswick Township. Medina attorney William G. Batchelder Jr., the father of the future 101st speaker of the Ohio House of Representatives and nearly forty-year state legislator William G. Batchelder III, sided with Elmer Eyssen and his township neighbors who were offended by the garbage-fed pig farm. Other leading members of Brunswick and Hinckley joined in the criticisms of not only the board of health but also Prosecutor Snedden. As a prominent businessman, Harry F. Gray asked *Medina County Gazette* readers, "Where is their loyalty?"

Initially, Prosecutor Snedden had advised the Medina County Board of Health that they were not legally required to take any actions in response to these residential complaints. Many citizens challenged that opinion, citing actions of the Cuyahoga County prosecutor against other garbage-fed pig farms in that adjoining county. Some asked why the Medina County officials failed to act. The Ohio Public Health Council and state health director would, in a short time, rule otherwise. The Medina Health Board would eventually act on the side of public health, but the political "black eye" for county officials was evident to many.[166]

Batchelder chose to run against a fellow Republican and incumbent Medina County prosecutor in the 1940 primary election, as did Republican David D. Porter, a former Medina County prosecutor. It's possible they smelled political blood in the water, or maybe not. Regardless, Prosecutor Snedden was vulnerable for more than one reason.

Newspaper accounts attributed some of Snedden's loss to Republicans' disdain for third terms. Republic officeholders for county engineer and a commissioner who were also seeking third terms, likewise, lost Republican support in the 1940 primary election. "Anti–third terms for incumbents," as a campaign theme, was very popular among Republicans in 1940, as they were preparing for a national presidential race in November against Franklin D. Roosevelt, who was also seeking an unprecedented third term.

The 1940 Republican primary results revealed that Batchelder's strongest support was primarily located in the Medina area, while the incumbent's strength was largely located in Wadsworth and Lodi. Countywide, Batchelder polled at 38 percent, while Snedden drew 33 percent and Porter gained a respectable 29 percent of the Republican voters. Not surprisingly, Prosecutor Snedden came in third in Brunswick Township with only 29 percent of the vote. Snedden and Porter were experienced attorneys and spent some years serving as appointed village solicitors. Batchelder, who had only passed the bar in June 1939, won on an advertised platform advocating for the benefits of youthful attorneys and suspicions of incumbents seeking third terms. Additionally, as his political advertisement stressed, "Nominate the man who is not connected with any pressure group or political machine, a Republican in the best sense of the word."[167]

The rancor and controversy over the pig farm in Brunswick undoubtedly hurt Prosecutor Snedden, thereby helping his opponents. Speaker Batchelder told me several years ago, when parts of this story first appeared in *Helping Hands* newsletter, that his father developed a friendship over this issue with Elmer Eyssen and some of his neighbors that would last for years to come. As the reader will note in a subsequent chapter, William G. Batchelder Jr. would go on to legally represent Brunswick Township residents as a private attorney in their annexation and public water fights with Brunswick City in the 1960s and 1970s.

William G. Batchelder Jr. would serve as the Medina County prosecutor from 1941 to 1953; he would also work in various local civic and political party positions and help found a generation of political and judicial leaders. Aside from his son's rise to the speakership, his daughter in-law Alice would be appointed to the United State District Court for the Northern District of Ohio and the Court of Appeals for the Sixth Circuit. Batchelder's sudden rise to county office and his family's involvement in local, county and state politics may owe something to a smelly hog farm in Brunswick. Who knows, if not for that controversy and vulnerability of the incumbent prosecutor, maybe the newcomer Batchelder would not have fared so well. In politics, you never know if the smells of controversy will breed a victory or defeat, but inevitably, it all remains subject to the winds of change.[168]

Guards Sign In Pig Feud

With a billboard advertising the county as "the home of the garbage-fed hog" and "a garbage dumping ground," a Medina, Ohio, estate owner Thursday protested against the odors of a nearby pig farm. He posted the man with the shotgun to see no one molested the sign. —(AP Wirephoto.

Guarding a controversial billboard while simultaneously exercising at least two fundamental constitutional rights—the First and Second Amendments. *From the Courier-Journal (Kentucky) January 20, 1939, 10.*

Public Health Service's so-called G-Men of science started warning in the 1930s that garbage-fed hogs had three times as many trichinae parasites as grain-fed hogs. They further warned that 80 percent of hog cholera could be directly traced to garbage feeding. Garbage feeding without controls constituted a major public health risk.

However, city garbage had to be dumped somewhere, and farmers during the Great Depression welcomed the steady cash for providing such disposal services. Cities and farmers were admittedly resistant to the notion that more expensive solutions were on the horizon. Akron mayor Lee Schroy complained in early 1939 that the drive to wipe out garbage-fed pig farms by the U.S. Public Health Service and the state board of health was going to put the city in a costly and untenable position. Feeding pigs garbage on a farm way out in the country was far cheaper than constructing a new incinerator, argued Mayor Schroy.[169]

The future site of scenic Mapleside Farms is a notable and historic landmark, displaying the pressures that made great changes in public sanitation. Citizens like Elmer Eyssen and local officials forced the issue to take necessary actions to abate the problem. While it was maybe a little embarrassing to the civic and commercial community, Eyssen's tactics heralded changes in leadership and the mindset of the community. While the incident has been long forgotten, that part of the county has enjoyed a close relationship with commercial agritourism. Had Eyssen's exercise of their constitutional rights not made such a public impact—embarrassing or not—maybe the garbage-fed-hog and garbage disposal methods would have prevailed awhile longer. The sights, sounds and smells of the farm that is now Medina's no. 1 tourist attraction are quite an improvement over those of the 1939 farm, thanks to public pressure and a little nationwide publicity.

23

1949

The Great Oleomargarine Debate and Citizen Initiative Petitions

*W*hat color should store-bought oleomargarine be? For those of us born after World War II, yellow is the first if not seemingly indisputable response. Nevertheless, back in 1949, Ohio voters had to answer that question at the ballot box. It was an important enough question to resolve that it led to a citizen initiative petition enacting a state law that the Ohio General Assembly refused to act on. The general assembly, as the *Akron Beacon Journal* argued at the time, had twice refused to alter an archaic law to ensure free competition between butter and margarine because of powerful dairy interests. Praising the citizens, the *Journal*'s editorial pointed out that they had rightly demanded reconsideration of the issue through the initiative petition.[170]

On Election Day, the proposed state statute permitting the manufacture and sale of colored oleomargarine passed, with 62 percent in favor. Despite statewide approval, the colored oleomargarine referendum failed in Medina County, with 53 percent opposed—largely because of the rural vote. Medina Village and Wadsworth were decisively in favor, with 62 percent and 66 percent in favor, respectively, but the opposition of the farmer vote in the rural townships outweighed the townspeople. Challenging the farmers' perspective, the *Medina Gazette* editorial opined before the vote, "Waving aside all the ballyhoo propounded by both sides, it appears to us that it all boils down to the question of whether or not the dairy industry is to have exclusive right to butter's traditional yellow color."[171]

Was it really about the color yellow or was it something else more significant? Fundamentally, the oleomargarine referendum issue repealed a state statute dating back to 1890 that protected the dairy industry, which argued in favor of consumer protection against "counterfeit butter." Ohio's approach was to require that oleomargarine be sold without coloring, thereby reducing its visual appeal. Some oleomargarine manufacturers compensated by including a yellow coloring agent to be mixed into the white mass of lard at home before consumption. Yum!

Ohio was not the only place where the great oleomargarine debate occurred. Invented in France around 1869, the new product found favor from Chicago meatpackers in the 1870s, as they were eager to capitalize on harvesting excess animal fat that had earlier been discarded. It became popular among millions of consumers who could not afford real butter during tough economic times. It was an obvious threat to the dairy industry. Congress took action in 1886 to arguably safeguard consumers, as well as dairy interests, by imposing a tax. The oleomargarine tax remained, although it was occasionally raised or challenged depending on the political whims of national politics, until 1950, when it was finally repealed.

Some historians have pointed out that changes in the manufacturing process and the inclusion of more farm crops in the ingredients of oleomargarine weakened the monolithic viewpoint of the dairy industry. Others have said that the inevitable political power of the urban working class likewise doomed the dominance of rural interests in both Washington, D.C., and Columbus. Despite the federal taxes and the inconvenience of mixing a coloring agent in the white lard, margarine sales grew because of

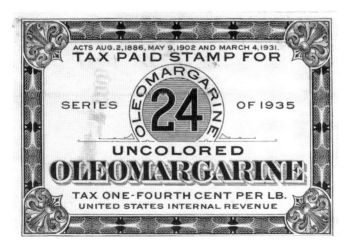

An uncolored Oleomargarine U.S. tax stamp from 1935 that cost one-fourth of a cent per pound for twenty-four pounds. *Author's collection.*

Congressional acts in 1886, 1902 and 1931 continued levying a special tax on uncolored oleomargarine, which remained in place until 1950. By 1902, thirty-two states regulated the color of oleomargarine sold by manufacturers and vendors to likewise protect dairy farming interests. The retail customers were provided with a yellow coloring agent to mix with the white mass to produce an aesthetically more pleasing product. In 1902, Congress also enacted a ten-cent-per-pound tax on colored oleomargarine and reduced the tax on uncolored margarine to be one-fourth of a cent per pound. Of special note is that oleomargarine destined for exportation was exempt from the tax. While the original premise of the taxes and regulations on oleomargarine was to purportedly protect consumers, that apparently didn't apply to foreign markets.

consumer demand for a cheaper substitute for butter. Because of Ohio's constitutional right for citizens to initiate petitions at the state level, the question was finally put to rest in the 1949 general election.[172]

There is an old saying that one should always know which side your bread is buttered on. Maybe the lesson to be learned from the great oleomargarine debate is that despite which side you think your own bread is buttered on, our system of state government is designed so that the voters will and should eventually prevail in answering those kinds of questions. In the end, some would offer that it's the "bread and butter" issues—regardless of how you color it—that really matter the most and in which the people will ultimately have their say at the ballot box.

BRUNSWICK "FUEDIN FARMERS" CONTINUES

Explosive Population Growth Drove Changes and Continuing Conflict

As the Brunswick "fuedin' farmers" of 1939 between a pig farmer and his neighbors drew nationwide attention, the community dispute foretold of the seemingly timeless story of conflict created by change. The "fuedin' farmers" tale reemerged in the 1950s and 1960s, again driven by widespread change in people and land use. In the 1950s, the growth of large-scale manufacturing in the region drew people from all over the United States to the area. New housing developments sprung up in southern Cuyahoga County and Brunswick Township.

YEAR MOVED INTO PRESENT HOUSE IN 1960

1959 to 1960	14,787	23%
1958	7,777	12%
1957	7,784	12%
1954 to 1956	12,727	19%
1950 to 1953	7,968	12%
1940 to 1949	7,956	12%
1939 or earlier	3,859	6%
Always Lived in House	2,457	4%
Medina County Total Population	**65,315**	**100%**

From 1950 to 1960, the total population of Medina County grew from 40,417 to 65,315, a 62 percent increase—the largest numerically when compared to any prior decade. As the table on the previous page details, by 1960, 78 percent of the people who moved into their homes had done so in the 1950s. Imagine living in Medina County in 1950 and then a decade later seeing that nearly eight out of every ten families you met at the stores, churches and school events were new to Medina County. How unsettling for county folk renowned for relatively prosperous farms and quaint village life.

Realty companies and homebuilders were increasingly abundant and prosperous in post–World War II northeast Ohio. New homes were being built at a prodigious rate, and people were moving into Medina County in droves. New home construction was accelerating as demands for public utility services, like water and sewer, were likewise increased to keep home prices low and property size within market expectations.

Typical post–World War II suburban homes in Brunswick offered spacious living rooms, a modern family-sized kitchen with a dining room, three bedrooms, a bath and shower space and a full basement on small lots (eighty-five by two hundred feet), with natural gas heat for less than $15,100, along with access to GI Bill–approved financing. In comparison, the average weekly earnings for a manufacturing worker in Ohio in 1957 was $93.36, around $4,855 per year. The national average cost for a new 1,138-square-foot single-family home was $10,000, not including land, heating equipment or the builder's development of financing costs. The average cost for the same home in the Cleveland area in 1959 was $13,109. The new homes in Brunswick were affordable for most middle-class families supported by their factory worker parents at the nearby Chevrolet and Ford plants.[173]

New-home construction accelerated the disputes between farmers and large property owners. New houses demand public services—public sewers and water systems mean that residential subdivisions can be built at a much higher density, and therefore, the land per acre is far more valuable. Farmers who wanted to sell even a few lots saw the financial desirability of city life. The farmers who wanted to remain in agriculture were generally opposed to the increased costs and the city dwellers who were hostile to the smells and traffic of country living. As Brunswick farmer Harper reminded us in our prior 1939 story, "Pigs is pigs, and this country around here is strictly farmland." While his first point was still correct in the 1950s, the latter was not for the Brunswick community.

In 1955, the Cleveland-based Alex and Fred Franklin Brothers Realty Company announced a $5 million low-cost housing development in the heart of Brunswick Township. Involving the construction of 410 homes, ranging in price from $10,000 to $14,000, it was promoted as one of the largest communities of its kind in northeast Ohio. Positioned on a ninety-seven-acre tract on State Route 303, just east of the center and the new elementary and high school buildings, the project also included a developer-built sewage treatment plant and public water system. In an agreement with county commissioners, both systems were to be turned over to the county on completion of the development.[174]

This was the pattern of development for much of the area in the 1950s—realty companies acquired large tracts of farmland, built the affordably priced homes on small lots surrounded by networks of paved streets and developer-constructed public utilities. If public water and sewer systems were not already available, developers built them as part of the development and then turned them over to the county. The supply of public water and sewer services became issues for the county, which eventually required the county commissioners to take action.

In late 1959, the Tri-County Planning Commission released a water supply report for Brunswick Township. It recommended that the commissioners negotiate with Cleveland for the sale of water to the area and form a sewer district for the entire drainage area of the Rocky River Basin within Medina County. In effect, the commissioners would have the legal authority to plan, oversee and operate public water systems and take over maintenance of the many small sewage plants being turned over to the county from developers.[175]

For Brunswick Township, a development such as this was under the purview and jurisdiction of the county commissioners until such a time that the area could incorporate as a municipality—a village or city. The area was not incorporated as a village until 1960. Following four prior attempts, voters approved, on November 3, 1959, the creation of Brunswick Village. It was to be formed from Brunswick Township land, making it twenty-five miles square—but only temporarily. State law allowed for village property owners to petition for detachments of large parcels from the municipality. At that point, led by farmers and other large property owners, a series of petition drives and local referendums successfully seceded thousands of acres of land from Brunswick Village and formed the newest and youngest township in Medina County: Brunswick Hills Township. Many of the petitioners argued that the higher taxes needed to finance a municipal government were their major concerns.[176]

Throughout the first half of 1960, feuding farmers, large property owners and others took advantage of a provision in state law that allowed detachments from the village to join the newly formed township. Three successive secession movements in 1960 divided the once-united community into two legal entities: township and village. Only the residents within the detached property were permitted to vote, not the entire village citizenry or their council. By the time Brunswick was officially declared a city and therefore no longer subject to detachments without a vote of council, three large areas were successfully detached. Once twenty-five miles square, the detachments brought the village's size down to 8 square miles, with eighty-eight different boundaries, creating confusion in safety and public services as well as a community divided. Public disputes and even a few private fights broke out between officials and residents over fire and police protection, street maintenance and water.[177]

1960 SECESSION VOTES FROM BRUNSWICK VILLAGE*

Date of Election	Acres to Secede	Yes Votes	No Votes	% Voting Yes
February 9, 1960	2,000	296	52	85%
April 26, 1960	2,000	58	12	83%
June 14, 1960	1,900	171	60	74%

*Only voters living in the area petitioning to secede were eligible to vote.

"Brunswick Must Find Water" was the headline of the *Akron Beacon Journal*, as the water from three wells in the Franklin brothers' allotment in Southeast Brunswick was projected to run out within five years. The Ohio Water Division warned the new city that the underground system, which was only producing 108,000 gallons per day peak, was maxing out. Other sources, like the Cleveland Water System, were being sought after, while the law director was urging that new building permits for homes be denied until a solution was obtained.[178]

Brunswick City officials acted accordingly and reached an agreement with the City of Cleveland to acquire bulk water and construct a municipal water system. Funding came from a 3.9 mill, thirty-year property tax levy to pay back a $1.2 million bond issue approved by Brunswick City voters in November 1962, with a vote of 2,289 to 777. With an estimated total cost of $3.4 million, the remainder of the project was funded by $1.9 million in special property tax assessments on all benefiting properties. All property owners in the city paid something to share the cost of a public water system,

1960

1964

1971

Brunswick City's boundaries changed dramatically from 1960 to 1971. *Courtesy of the Medina County Highway Engineer.*

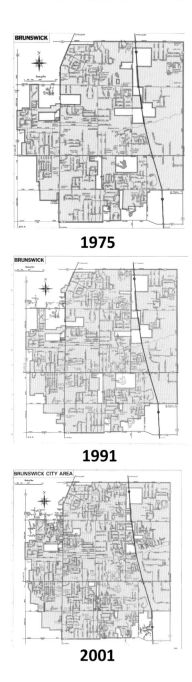

1975

1991

2001

Brunswick City boundaries from 1975 to 2001. Note the
continuing decline of the "township islands" that were
surrounded by property located within city boundaries.
Courtesy of the Medina County Highway Engineer.

while users paid more based on finance costs and the amount of water used. Those in the township, even if they were surrounded by property in the city, paid nothing but could not have access to the city water, according to Brunswick City officials—that is, unless they annexed and reattached to the city, thereby sharing in the costs of the water system improvements.[179]

The availability of the water meant there was a renewed interest in residential building in Brunswick. A series of annexation proceedings occurred rapidly over the next several years and into the subsequent decades. From 1964 to mid-1966, an estimated 1,200 acres were annexed back into the municipal corporation. From then on, as seen in the images on page 149 and 150, the large islands and peninsulas of township property were eventually annexed back into the city.

All of this set up the conditions for the division and conflict that has remained for over six decades—between township and city residents, between farmers and large property owners wanting different uses and futures for their land and between the city and the county. The county retained control of the sewers in the area through the sanitary sewer districts. The City of Brunswick and the City of Cleveland, by proxy, took over control of the water systems within the municipal boundaries and any newly annexed properties from the township.

The county commissioners retained control of future water services in the township and developed a water system for northwestern Medina County. Water was obtained from the Avon Lake Water Treatment Plant via Rural Lorain County Water Authority. Currently, the water is conveyed through three separate locations that can deliver 14 million gallons per day to a massive system of pipes, water storage tanks and water pumping stations, serving approximately 15,275 customers. For the Brunswick area, its proposed construction in the 1970s competed with the City of Brunswick, but over the past decades, service agreements have been painfully enacted.

Eventually, conflicts over the new system expansion and services, often intertwined with disputes over annexed property, resulted in various lawsuits. An eventually meaningful compromise between the parties was accomplished before the Medina County Common Pleas Court in 1977. In what is referred to as a "Journal Entry to Case Number 30174," the City of Brunswick and Medina County commissioners designated various areas for future water services essentially based on economics and engineering, as well as the wishes of effected property owners.[180]

Regardless, over the last sixty years of disputes involving the City of Brunswick, Brunswick Hills Township and Medina County commissioners

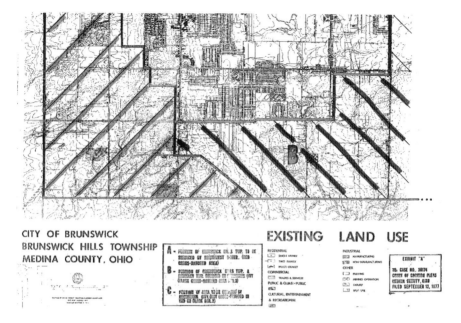

A water service agreement map: exhibit A, in Medina County Common Pleas Court Case no. 30174 between Medina County commissioners and the City of Brunswick. *Courtesy of the Medina County Commissioners Office.*

over competing land use and access to water, there has been undeniable consistency—tension-filled but consistent. As Brunswick Hills Township's land gets reattached to the municipality and the jurisdiction gets smaller in size and its property tax base lessens, the city gets closer to its original size. Even though its return to a single community twenty-five miles square will never likely happen, the consistency of the arguments remains.

The City of Brunswick has consistently maintained that access to public water comes only with annexation to the city—with few exceptions. The Brunswick Hills Township officials consistently oppose annexations of land to the city—with few exceptions. The third party in the conflict, the property owners, consistently want what is best for them and their investment, often involving water and public services—with few exceptions.

The Medina County commissioners consistently try to balance between the competing political expectations of the township and city officials and those of the property owners. All of this is within the purview and guidance of state laws. To this day, one additional characteristic remains: although the farmers have all but disappeared in Brunswick's annexation requests, in the 2020s, it is the "fuedin'" over water, city boundaries and future land use that continues. It is a consistency many would rather see fade away.

25

MAKING OHIO'S STATE SEAL UNIQUE POST-1967

Each state in the Union has an official seal that serves both emblematic and functional purposes. They are often designed to represent a state's history, origins or great triumphs. Functionally, they also designate that a legal or government document has been created or sanctioned under state authority.

Ohio's seal and related coat of arms has an interesting history, as it has been redesigned at least ten different times since the formation of the state in 1803. From 1805 to 1866, the design was left unspecified by the general assembly, a unique situation among the states. Prior to 1967, the requirements called for the following: "In the background, and rising above the sheaf and arrows, a mountain range over which appears a rising sun." But other design elements were added on occasion. Over several decades, for example, Ohio's seal had a canal boat along with the aforementioned background. In fact, that "canal boat" state seal, created in 1841, was placed in the 1861 statehouse rotunda skylight and is also found at the base of the Speaker's platform in the Ohio House of Representatives. The Ohio Canal era and associated public works and civil engineering triumphs were truly historic achievements of the state. However, the benefits as well as economic viability barely lasted the rest of the nineteenth century due to the emergence of the steam railroad industry. Consequently, the canal boat was dropped from the seal by the 1870s.

In 1967, a visual depiction of the seal was officially standardized by the Ohio General Assembly. The design required representations of Mount

Logan in Chillicothe and the Scioto River, uniting the background and foreground; cultivated fields and a sheaf of wheat to represent Ohio's substantial agricultural presence; and a bundle of arrows to commemorate the Native predecessors of the land.

While Ohio's seal is attractive, it is not unique. At least eight states have arrows on their seal, another ten states have sheaves of wheat, fourteen states have a rising sun and Ohio is not well known for its mountain ranges. Respecting the origin of the seal design, Representative Rick Perales (R-Seventy-Third District) sponsored House Bill 370 in the 132nd General Assembly, which would have added a design element that recognizes a unique contribution to human history attributable to Ohio's own: the Wright brothers. His bill would have added a depiction of the Wright brothers' flyer to the seal in recognition of their great achievement in applying the scientific method, intellectual interests and ceaseless curiosity to build the first aircraft and introduce a new era in the history of man. On February 12, 2018, it passed the Ohio House of Representatives by a vote of 90 to 3 and had 74 house cosponsors, but unfortunately, it only had one hearing in the Ohio Senate Government Oversight and Reform Committee and therefore died at the end of the session.

There is a Medina County connection to the story of the first flight. It has often been repeated by the local A.I. Root Company of Medina and shared nationally in *The Wright Brothers* by David McCullough. The progenitor of "America's first family in beekeeping" was the only eyewitness to publish national articles about successful airplane flights made by the Wright brothers in Ohio in 1904–5. A.I. Root was a trusted friend and visited the brothers' workshop and testing grounds at Huffman Prairie, near Dayton, in 1904. He drove his own automobile, an Oldsmobile Runabout, over two hundred miles from Medina to Dayton in what must have been a remarkable journey itself, given the nature of public roadways at the time.[181]

A.I. Root's enthusiasm for the eventual effect of what the Wright brothers had accomplished was evident in his accounts. Few other discoveries in human history have exceeded the beneficial impact of these brothers from Ohio. In the 132nd General Assembly, HB-370 sought to make sure Ohio took rightful action to stake that claim amid a frequent assertion by the state of North Carolina, the home of Kitty Hawk, as the "birthplace of flight." The skies of North Carolina's beaches were an important factor in testing the Wright brothers' early design work and engineering skills. However, it was the genius of the Ohio entrepreneurs that made the day—North Carolina just provided the windy beach.

Top, left: An 1849 seal prominently depicting a canal boat along with bundles of grains and arrows in front of a mountainous landscape. *From the Ohio Statehouse Gallery display* Great Seals of the State of Ohio; *photograph taken by the author*.

Top, right: A 1966 version of the great seal of the State of Ohio (prior to standardization on December 15, 1967). *From the* Ohio House of Representatives Membership Directory *(Columbus: State of Ohio, 1966)*.

Bottom, left: A proposed standardized design of the state seal with the Wright brothers' flyer was presented at the Ohio House State and Local Government Committee by bill sponsor Representative Rick Perales in 2017. The author was present. *Photograph from the Ohio House of Representatives, District 69 Office*.

Bottom, right: The 1967 standardized version that was adopted. *From the Ohio Statehouse Gallery display* Great Seals of the State of Ohio; *photograph taken by the author*.

American poet laureate James Dickey once observed, "Flight is the only truly new sensation that men have achieved in modern history." Perhaps there will be a time when the Ohio seal officially recognizes the claim to that engineering and scientific marvel. It will serve as a reminder to the world that Ohio is not just the birthplace of a couple of presidents but also the home of industrious entrepreneurs that changed the history of mankind for all time.

DISAGREEMENT OVER COURTHOUSE DESIGN IS NOTHING NEW

*A*n old saying goes, "Be careful what you wish for, you might just get it." The first recorded controversy of a courthouse design in Medina County was set in motion by the Ohio General Assembly and Governor Rhodes in July 1965, when they created a second common pleas judgeship. Not only supporting a new judgeship, but also advocating for it before the legislature were Medina County common pleas judge Windsor Kellogg, Wadsworth solicitor Charles Johnston Jr., Medina County Bar Association president and county prosecutor James Foreman and Bar Association Common Pleas Committee chairman William G. Batchelder Jr. Also included as supporters were Probate Judge Wayne Garver, State Representative H. Dennis Dannley and County Commissioners Joseph Neath, Howard Dunn and Kenneth Indoe. The explosive growth of court cases and population in Medina County mandated it, they argued. However, where to fit a courtroom, offices and jury room into an already cramped courthouse was a major problem—as was the expense.[182]

The county commissioners were required by state law to provide a courtroom and supporting facilities for the second judge. Being a bit short on cash, they contended that it was far better to have a short one mill levy than borrow and pay for twenty years of interest. The commissioners asked for the assistance of the Medina Bar Association, as well as the effected county officials, on the concept design and layout of the new courthouse. By February 1966, architect William Boyd Huff and associates from Akron, who had also designed the county jail on East Liberty Street, provided sketches of a proposed courthouse expansion. Connecting the old courthouse with

The "old" 1841 courthouse. *Courtesy of the Medina County Historical Society.*

the jail was proposed to be a "slick, three-story glass brick and metal panel building....The building will be taller and different in style and materials. The latter two bar brick buildings, simply but attractively ornamented with stone window trim."[183]

The modern design may have been compatible with the jail. However, it was not deemed by many of the public to be compatible with the 1873 French Second Empire façade of the old courthouse, nor was it in keeping with a growing preference within Medina for a more historic, colonial Western Reserve look. Following a fury of public outcry by citizens, elected officials, a newly formed Medina Community Design Committee and local historical societies that oversaw the first design, the architect redesigned the buildings in both contemporary and colonial architectural styles. On June 21, 1966, the proposed courthouse addition plans and project phases were revealed to the public, and their opinions were invited.[184]

Commissioner Chairman Joseph Neath reported that 95 percent of those who attended the public viewing of the courthouse design favorably accepted the "colonial architecture" referred to in the press as Toscan Roman. Reportedly, Probate Judge Wayne Garver and County Recorder Elsie Fetzer preferred the contemporary design instead because of its considerable savings to the costs by eliminating the columns at the entrance.

The 1969 courthouse with its selected Toscan Roman architecture. *This photograph was taken by the author in 2010.*

Placed on the general election ballot in November 1966, a one mill levy to build a new courthouse overwhelmingly lost in every community but one township, with 68 percent countywide voting "no." The worst showing was in Brunswick City, with 82 percent opposed. Although it was endorsed by the *Medina County Gazette* and pretty much every civic leader who had advocated for the new judgeship, it probably lost for at least two reasons. Many complained that the commissioners had paid too much for the property, while others suggested that too many other competing money issues were on the ballot at the same time. Conventional wisdom is that voters typically need at least three reasons to vote in favor of a money issue and only one reason to vote against. Apparently, nearly seven out of ten voters found that one reason to vote no. Commissioners were then forced to finance the project by issuing $1.5 million worth of twenty-year general obligation bonds pledging future general funds.[185]

State law clearly asserts that when, in the board of county commissioners' judgment, a courthouse is needed, the buildings and offices shall be of such style, dimensions and expense as the board determines (Ohio Revised Code 307.01). Despite the failure of the tax levy at the ballot box, on December 15, 1966, county commissioners and judges decided the courthouse addition would be started immediately. In a prepared statement, the county

A 1946 postcard of the Wood County, Ohio Courthouse. Author's collection.

commissioners said: "The county does not contemplate any revision of the exterior of the existing courthouse, and the exterior of the new building will be constructed to harmonize with the courthouse and will enhance the appearance of the public square and the surrounding real estate."

It took all of 1967 and 1968 to purchase the adjoining properties, design the final structure, bid out and build the "new" courthouse. On January 12, 1969, a formal dedication was held, with Medina's native son and Lieutenant Governor John Brown as the master of ceremonies and Ohio Supreme Court justice Louis Schneider as the keynote speaker.[186]

A state legislator and former county commissioner once offered some advice to me that may be relevant: if you can avoid it, don't get involved in a new courthouse or addition project. No matter what, everybody seems to have an opinion that usually bears little relationship with expertise in courthouse design or their frequency of use. Nobody wants to really pay for it, and most will say they like it just the way it is. The saving grace is if you do your job right, eventually, almost everybody will like the changes, and in a few years, most people will not even understand or remember the fight. That seems to be the case for the "new" Medina Courthouse, finished in 1969. As for its currently proposed replacement, under construction in 2021, that remains to be seen.

WOOD COUNTY COURTHOUSE: A CONTROVERSY THAT LED ALL THE WAY TO THE OHIO SUPREME COURT

The Wood County Courthouse was constructed amid a slew of indictments of county commissioners, architects and contractors involved in the project. Regardless of the guilt or innocence of those charged, the county prosecutor later explained: "The people of this county were very angry at that time because the courthouse was being built without a vote of the people, and they were ready to find an indictment against every person who had anything to do with the courthouse" (*Marion Star*, "Yost and Packard Exonerated," February 29, 1896, 1).

On June 27, 1895, three commissioners were found guilty of misconduct in office in employing the courthouse architect without acting in conjunction with a building committee that had been appointed by circuit judges to oversee the project. The judge removed two commissioners from office on July 20, 1895, but the Ohio Supreme Court reversed the convictions the following March 31. Despite these traumatic events, the massive sandstone courthouse in the Richardsonian Romanesque style is considered one of the finest in Ohio and a historic landmark.[187]

MEDINA COUNTY VOTER INSIGHT ON TAXES IS ALWAYS IMPORTANT

*G*iving public officials the authority to raise taxes without requiring a vote of the electorate has typically been a complicated and controversial issue throughout the history of Ohio. On one side, the traditional argument has been that elected officials need to be authorized to perform some basic functions of government—spend, borrow, enact fees for services and tax—with reasonable restraints and the eventual reckoning for their performance at the polls. On the other side, there has been an antitax streak in the American culture dating back to the nation's founding. The axiomatic writing of U.S. Supreme Court chief justice John Marshall in *McCulloch v. Maryland*, "the power to tax involves the power to destroy," articulates the underlying fear that compels restrictions on that authority. Hence, Ohio law has frequently balanced these ongoing and seemingly irretractable but important differences.

Provisions of the Ohio Constitution adopted in 1912 prohibit the general assembly from putting statewide tax issues on the ballot, except for those that directly fund public education. However, over the last century, the legislature has consistently passed laws that limit the ability of local and county governments to enact various taxes—income, sales, lodging and property—without submitting them for voter approval. The debate continues to rage between the two opposing viewpoints, thus affecting local and county public finances.

In Medina County, since the 1960s, driven largely by our robust population growth and a demand for more public services, we have seen this debate with some regularity, as critical county projects frequently come down to borrowing versus increasing tax revenues. Despite losing a requested $1 million tax increase at the ballot box in 1966 (68 percent countywide opposing), the commissioners pushed forward with constructing the 1969 courthouse by borrowing $1.5 million. Unfortunately, by 1971, plagued by a succession of eighteen months of deficit spending—largely impacted by the costs of the new courthouse project, judges and the sheriff departments— county commissioners were forced to pass a 0.5 percent "piggyback" sales tax starting on April 1. Over a five-year period, court budgets had increased 196 percent, and the sheriff's budget had increased by 76 percent. Generally, the other costs of county government were rapidly rising as well, while revenues comprised almost entirely of property taxes grew at a much slower pace.

The three county commissioners—John Oberholtzer (D), Charles Clark (R) and Kenneth Indoe (R)—all voted in favor of the "piggyback" sales tax as an emergency, which meant it took effect immediately. Even after five well-attended public hearings before enacting the tax, the commissioners caught the opposition off-guard by passing it as an emergency, thereby changing the referendum petition language needed to force a vote on the issue. Opponents of the sales tax, in their haste, filed the wrong petition form and were denied the ability to place it on the 1971 ballot. While leaders of the repeal effort promised to return with the proper referendum petitions in early 1972, they never materialized. One of the commissioners who voted for the tax, Charles Clark, chose to run for reelection in 1972; he was easily renominated by the Republican Party and reelected in November 1972. Indoe chose not to run, and voters chose to replace him with Republican Don Simmons.

In June 1991, the county commissioners, by a two-to-one vote, enacted a 0.5 percent sales tax increase for three and a half years to fund a Medina County Justice Center. However, a citizens' campaign led by the county auditor gathered over 6,200 signatures and forced the issue on the ballot. Despite bipartisan support (Democrat sheriff and two Republican commissioners) for the temporary increase, the issue went down, with 56 percent opposing. Much of the political debate over the issue in 1991 and a subsequent commissioners race in 1992 came down to the decision of whether to enact the tax without a vote of the people. It was a political lesson learned by many at the time: just because you have the authority to enact the tax without a referendum doesn't mean you should.

In recent years, legislation in the Ohio General Assembly has been proposed to effectively place into law what the political culture of Medina

County has already demonstrated: don't increase taxes unless you get voter approval first. However, if enacted, it would have a profound effect on Medina County's bond rating, credit rating and the cost of borrowing. Higher bond ratings mean a lower cost of borrowing, just like your typical consumer loan. In 2018, S&P Global Ratings raised its rating on Medina County's general obligation debt to AA+ from AA for a number of reasons. One of the major factors listed was the ability of the county to raise the sales tax 0.5 percent without voter approval. In the event of a fiscal emergency, like a major economic downturn or another drastic cut in state funding, the county commissioners could then enact such a tax increase—even temporarily—to make certain that the legally required debts or bonds are paid. Clearly, just having the authority but not exercising it has a significant and measurable financial benefit to the county.

Our system was designed to be a representative democracy in which the voters regularly weigh in at the ballot box while elected officials are given specific but fairly expansive authority to act on behalf of the public on a wide range of matters. In my experience, Medina County has a proud tradition of voter involvement that every elected official recognizes. Our history is replete with examples of what Ronald Reagan once said: "When you can't make them see the light, make them feel the heat." I am thankful that in Medina County, the "light" from voter insight is usually enough.

Passing On the Lessons We Learned

Vietnam War Memorial

*E*very war that the United States had waged over its history as a nation has a different story. The lessons that a generation has learned from those wars, likewise, have varied, but all of them are important for the succeeding generations to listen to, remember and, most important of all, heed. The lessons of the Vietnam War are no less important than those of the more recent or even more distant national struggles. However, the insight of the Vietnam War generation, which experienced firsthand the blood, sweat and tears of the sacrifices made and the promises broken, are in the twilight of departing from the national consciousness forever. Few of our current youth understand or even recognize the costs those Vietnam era youth who served in our military endured. It is hard to adequately describe nor possible to fully relate the feelings of distrust and turmoil that our society was undergoing at the time.

In 1989, the Vietnam War veterans in Medina County decided to build a special memorial to remember the thirty-three citizens who gave their lives in defense of our great nation in that unique struggle in Southeast Asia. That memorial was built on a grassy knoll overlooking the countryside on county property situated on Northland Drive in Medina City.

The dedication ceremonies were held on Memorial Day, May 27, 1990, with over one thousand people attending. Among them were the local American Legion, VFW and POW-MIA groups, as well as service organizations and various elected officials. The memorial was made possible by over $45,000 in donations from community members and businesses.

At the head of this noteworthy community effort was the Memorial Committee of the Vietnam Veterans of America, Medina County Chapter 385. In some small but meaningful way, it has become a way for that generation of veterans to reach out and implore the future generations of Medina County to remember those noble sacrifices for our freedoms.

On the day of the dedication, some of the most important lessons of the Vietnam War were no better articulated than by one of the war's veterans who led the effort to construct the memorial. Lou Becks, a chairman of the Memorial Committee of Vietnam Veterans of America, pleaded to those assembled: "Never ask men and women to serve in a war we do not intend to win." He observed, "We learned we should not enter a war unless it is necessary for our national survival. And if we do enter such a war, we must support our men and women to the fullest extent of our powers." Certainly, these are words worth remembering for those willing to listen and reflect on the human costs dearly sacrificed to give them meaning.

Twenty-eight years later, the Vietnam Veterans of America, Chapter 385, under the leadership of Rick Pethtel (a veteran of the U.S. Marine Corps), revisited the long-term preservation of the memorial. While the memorial took on an additional legacy of honoring all Medina County veterans, the weathering from many seasons also took its toll on the memorial's walls and pavers. Similarly, the membership of the 501(c)(3) nonprofit organization has weathered as many years and is slowly waning as

The "3" Design

The memorial's design incorporates the number three and combinations of that number whenever possible to honor the thirty-three Medina County men who lost their lives in the Republic of South Vietnam and surrounding areas. The memorial has:

- A three-sided main stone (thirty-three inches by seventy-two inches).
- A three-sided base stone (forty-five inches by twelve inches).
- A six-sided foundation stone (forty-eight inches by eighteen inches).
- Three benches, three bronze markers/U.S. flag groupings.
- Three sets of evergreens (each thirty-three inches tall).
- Of the twenty-eight designs submitted, elements from the submissions of John Lawrence, Tony Cerny, Chris Beck, Mike Buzzi and the Jason McCourt families were combined for the final result.

that generation passes on. With the intent of repairing and upgrading the memorial one last time and handing permanent ownership and upkeep to the Medina County Veterans Services Office, the group sought funding and donations of materials to complete the project in 2019.

In June 2019, Senator Larry Obhof, State Representative Darrell Kick and I were able to obtain a State of Ohio grant of $60,000 to match local funds and material donations in the costs of repairing and upgrading the Vietnam Memorial. New pavement bricks, a foundation with better drainage, upgraded LED lighting and new electrical wiring surrounds the memorial structure, designed to last several more generations of Medina County residents. To complete the project, Vietnam Veterans of America, Chapter 385, raised an additional $30,000 and following construction and upgrades, rededicated it on November 10, 2019, with appropriately 150 people in attendance.[188]

It has been said that no event in American history is more misunderstood or misreported than the Vietnam War. The veterans of that war who are living in Medina County asked that future generations don't forget the sacrifices that were made for their freedoms. The memorial, though only made of brick and stone, represents so much more. I am certain that it will remain a testament to the love of faith, family, community and country that is the history of the people living in Medina County.

SALES TAX FOR SCHOOLS

Good Thing Medina County Voters Didn't Wait
for a State Funding Fix

Medina County is the only county in the State of Ohio that has a county sales tax collected and dedicated to public schools, an amazing, significant and unique political event for the State of Ohio. So, how did it happen?

In the May 8, 2007 election, 56.5 percent of Medina County voters approved a 0.5 percent sales tax earmarked specifically for public school permanent improvements, the first of its kind in the state's history. The sales tax is for a thirty-year duration. These revenues can be used only for the purpose of school district permanent improvements within Medina County—not salaries or operating expenses.

The journey was not a smooth one. Summit County officials had tried in 2002 to pass a similar measure but failed, with 54 percent of voters opposed for a number of reasons. One significant issue that was not present in Medina County was the distrust between the big city school district of Akron and the surrounding communities. Some school district superintendents in Summit County reportedly held back public support in fear of endangering their own local funding issues.[189]

Another issue, present in both counties, was the general dissatisfaction of voters with the funding of public education by the State of Ohio. The Ohio Supreme Court had ruled three times in the 1990s DeRolph cases against the state's overreliance on property taxes to fund education, as well as the effects of the unequal distribution of property wealth. Disparate educational opportunities were evident because of the funding system and formula being used by the state. Many voters in both counties, reacting to the system inequities, voiced objections to county governments being involved in solving a funding issue that was essentially up to the state legislature to resolve.

School boards in Medina, looking for alternatives to funding for their districts, emerged from strategic planning sessions facilitated by the Medina County Educational Services Center superintendent Will Koran with formation of an Alternative Funding Study Committee. The study committee evaluated a number of options and, thereafter, produced a recommendation that would require the legal authority of the board of county commissioners to use state law in a fashion that had never been successfully accomplished. The proposal entailed the creation of a Community Improvement Board (CIB), which had the authority to distribute annual grants from the proceeds of an enacted 0.5 percent sales tax approved by the voters. These grants could only be used to fund permanent improvements—anything with a lifespan of over five years, according to state law—of public school districts. Teachers' salaries and operating expenses would not be eligible expenses.

At the time of the proposal, the legal authority to use a CIB and to enact a sales tax dedicated for school funding purposes was arguable. The Summit County initiatives had obtained a legal opinion from a private and prestigious Cleveland law firm, Squires, Sanders & Dempsey, that such a mechanism was legally possible. Medina County prosecutor Dean Holman publicly posed doubts about the ability of the board of county commissioners to limit the permanent improvements for school districts only. In addition, he questioned whether the commissioners could likewise limit the distribution of such funds in a predetermined manner to the various school districts. After considerable pressure from school officials and some county officials, the prosecutor submitted the questions to the Ohio attorney general Mark Dann for an official opinion.

Newly elected Attorney General Mark Dann officially issued Opinion No. 2007-002 on February 7, 2007, responding to the legal questions posed. First, the board of county commissioners could legally propose to Medina County voters a sales tax levy limited to permanent improvements for school districts only. Secondly, the commissioners could not restrict the CIB in defining how the proceeds would be distributed among the districts or what would be considered a permanent improvement.

The proponents of the "sales tax for schools" effort quickly responded. Before placing the issue on the ballot, the CIB was formed, and the commissioners encouraged the board to consider the distribution of the grants proportionally based on enrollment. The CIB then met on March 13, 2007, enacted regulations for the operation of the board and stipulating that the distribution of tax revenues would be on a proportional student enrollment basis.

Before the May election, all of the public school boards of Medina County formally met together in the Broadway Theater in the county administration building. They passed additional resolutions confirming a Memorandum of Understanding, pledging that no school district would apply for annual grants from the CIB that were not in accordance with its proportional share of students based on annual enrollment figures.

Based on the agreements between the commissioners, the CIB and all school boards, any changes to the distribution of the sales tax would have to be approved by the board of commissioners, the Community Improvement Board and a majority of the school districts. In effect, the voters were guaranteed that if they approved the sales tax increase, the tax levy would be distributed based on the student enrollment. Essentially, the money followed each child equally. Each district student was funded the same amount, regardless of which public school district they attended—this included students going to the Medina County Career Center, as well. In total, because of public school boundaries, a total of eleven districts receive proceeds from the sales tax based on their Medina County student enrollment. Importantly, the approved ballot language clearly stated that the additional revenues raised by the 0.5 percent sales tax increase was to be used exclusively for school districts within the county.

CONVINCING THE VOTERS

The campaign organization was unique, as it utilized the experienced volunteers and organizations of local district levy committees while coordinating the countywide messages and push for regional and countywide support. There was a central countywide committee called Keep Our Schools Excellent (KOSE) that developed the overall strategy, countywide messages, printing of signs, county literature advertising, and also charged with obtaining endorsements and fundraising. Each of the seven public school districts also formed their own district campaign committees to distribute the yard signs, run local public information campaigns, conduct door-to-door literature drops, organize local telephone banks and raise money for the campaign.

There were a number of strengths in the sales tax levy initiative that proved essential in passing the issue in Medina County and which didn't exist in the Summit County initiatives. There was a strong bipartisan non-school leadership at the county level in favor: a Democrat Medina County auditor joined with two Republican county commissioners to actively campaign in support of the issue. There was unanimous support among all seven boards of education, superintendents and local district campaign committees. The clear campaign message was this: this was a one-time-only proposal—there would be "no second chance" to provide local funding for education using the sales tax. Another strong message that resonated was that shoppers from outside Medina County would help pay the costs of school construction and permanent improvements. Lastly, the message of "Keep Our Schools Excellent" played off the singular distinction that all the districts in the county had been rated "excellent" by the Ohio Department of Education— the only county with that honor.

There was significant local newspaper support from the editors of the *Medina County Gazette* and the *Akron Beacon Journal*. However, an early criticism of the attempt by the *Cleveland Plain Dealer* endangered the campaign effort. The KOSE committee worked diligently to reverse the effects of the editorial, and after meeting with local officials, the editors fortunately reversed their opinion. It provided a much-needed boost in support while also revealing an injurious but non-lethal criticism. The *Plain Dealer* editorial board had originally advocated a "wait and see" what the state and Governor Strickland did to address school funding. As we all know, we are all still waiting for that state remedy to help Medina County schools.

In total, the sales tax issue was successful, with 56.5 percent of the county voting "yes." However, it failed in several of the school districts, in large part due to competing money issues on the ballot—$1.25 million Medina District Library Replacement Levy, Buckeye Schools 1 Percent Income Tax and Brunswick School District's $2.07 million replacement. The Brunswick Replacement levy passed with 53 percent of the vote, while the Buckeye 1 Percent Income Tax failed, with only 39 percent approving.

As seen in the table on the following page, the turnout varied from 19 percent to 39 percent, but the large-scale support within Highland Local (63 percent), Medina City Schools (61 percent) and Wadsworth City Schools (74 percent) overwhelmed the losses in the remaining four districts. The measure only had to win a majority countywide, not in every district. In the end, however, every school and student won with passage of the first and only sales tax for schools in the state of Ohio.

0.5% SALES TAX FOR SCHOOLS ISSUE PRIMARY ELECTION 2007

	Reg. Voters	Yes	No	% Yes	% Turnout
Brunswick City Schools	31,570	2,817	3,036	48%	19%
Buckeye Local	9,794	1,685	2,135	44%	39%
Black River Local	2,478	249	308	45%	22%
Cloverleaf Local	14,709	1,675	2,097	44%	26%
Highland Local	11,959	1,730	998	63%	23%
Medina City Schools	33,188	4,743	3,041	61%	23%
Wadsworth City Schools	19,261	4,047	1,433	74%	28%
Total	**122,959**	**16,946**	**13,048**	**56.5%**	**24.4%**

*Votes in precincts with multiple school districts were calculated into largest district.

Supporters saw the sales tax funding as a possible model for other districts across the state and nation. The collection of the new sales tax started October 1, while distribution of quarterly payments to all school districts on a per-student basis was initiated in 2008. Common purchases that were not subject to the new 0.5 percent sales and use tax included many household budget items. Exemptions from the tax were goods consumed off premises, such as groceries; prescription drugs and durable medical equipment; motor vehicle fuel (gasoline and diesel); items purchased with food stamps; newspaper and magazine subscriptions; and public utilities, like gas, water, sanitary sewer and electricity delivered through pipes, conduits or wires. At the time of the new 6.5 percent rate, fifty-two counties were still higher, seven lower and twenty-eight equal to Medina County.

The use of county authority to levy a sales and use tax is strongly guarded by county commissioners and other county officials. Because of the specific sections of the law that allowed the creation of a CIB and enactment of the sales tax are limited, currently, only forty-four out of eighty-eight counties have remaining authority. The County Commissioners Association of Ohio has taken a strong stance in their yearly legislative agenda opposed to the

A "sales tax for schools" campaign yard sign. *Author's collection.*

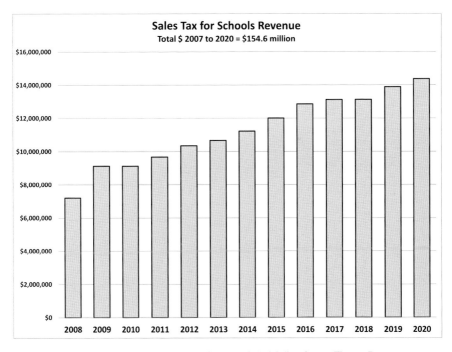

A "sales tax for schools" revenue history. *Courtesy of the Medina County Finance Department.*

use of any sales tax revenues for school purposes, regardless of the success in Medina County. Hence, the strong political objections throughout the state have hindered official efforts to try it in other counties. Discussion and proposals to attempt the same thing emerge every now and then in various counties in Ohio but always with the same stifling conclusions.

County commissioners who have the sales tax authority don't want to share the revenues with their school districts. After all, isn't that something the state legislature is supposed to fix? Maybe, but Medina County voters couldn't and didn't wait for the politicians in Columbus to finally and completely address the DeRolph decisions. The local school districts will always have to come up with local dollars to fund education. The question, which was asked during the campaign, was simply this: how do you want to fund a portion of the local share? For Medina County voters, the sales tax for schools was the answer.

30

RETURN TO NORMALCY

After the 1918 Spanish Flu and 2020 COVID-19 Pandemics

*A*mid the COVID-19 pandemic, the Ohio government and citizens reacted. Some reacted predictably, others less so. In addition to the weekly briefings of Governor DeWine, constant national news from the CDC and commentaries revolving around presidential campaign efforts, everybody was perpetually inundated with stories about the social, economic and political implications of the disease and government actions for months on end. Frequent comparisons were made to the Spanish flu of 1918–19. It was once called the mother of all pandemics because all influenza pandemics since that time were caused by descendants of the 1918 virus. However, the COVID-19 virus is a brand-new strain for humanity to deal with in the short term, as well as for the foreseeable future.

Until 2020, the 1918–19 influenza pandemic was the most severe in modern history. The pandemic spread, for the most part, concurrently in three distinct waves over twelve months in 1918–19 in Asia, Europe and North America. In total, the number of deaths was estimated to be at least 50 million worldwide and about 675,000 in the United States. For Medina County, the records show that the most deaths and illnesses attributed to the flu occurred in the fall of 1918 and the following spring of 1919. In fact, Medina health officer F.L. Harding had imposed varying restrictions on public meetings, public and private schools, theaters, restaurants, clubs and churches over an eight-week period.[190]

The approach in Ohio in 1918 was for the state department of health to encourage action by local officials to deal with the spreading disease instead of statewide mandates and business closings. Hence, not only were there varying rates of deaths and illness across the state, dependent on individual precautions, but there were also differing community actions. The impact on the economy was likewise varied. Large cities, like Cleveland, Cincinnati, Columbus, were harder hit with fatalities and cases than Medina County, but still, the local impact was significant in lives lost, illnesses and public activity diminished.

In Medina County, there were losses of life that were covered in front-page news articles relating the deaths of civic leaders and businessmen, while others maybe less renowned mentioned in various local community news. Almost all died in their homes or with family. In Medina County, Lodi and Wadsworth were the only communities with hospitals at the time. Back then, people who were stricken with a contagious disease were not supposed to go to the hospital; rather, they were supposed stay at home to recoup, recover or succumb to the complications of the disease—typically pneumonia.

Public health officials advocated for nonpharmaceutical precautions and treatment back then, just as they did early in the 2020 pandemic. Instructions from health officials sound familiar—they advised keeping clean hands, eating nourishing foods, staying at home and isolating away from other family members if one felt sick, protecting others by sneezing and coughing

CONFLICT BETWEEN THE LORD AND THE LAW?

A story from St. Louis reported in the *Mansfield News-Journal* at the time of the Spanish flu pandemic highlights the conflict between religious leaders and government officials that can sometimes occur. Apparently, a St. Louis preacher, while conducting a religious gathering, illegally disobeyed a health department order prohibiting children under sixteen years from attending. Despite a warning from a volunteer health inspector and later a policeman, the preacher persisted, was arrested and was shortly thereafter brought before the judge. In his defense of letting the children attend, Preacher Hutcherson stated, "The Lord says, 'Suffer little children to come unto me,' so I let them come in." The judge retorted, "Yes. True enough. But when the Lord said that, he didn't know anything about the 'flu.' Fifty dollars and costs."

Source: *Mansfield News-Journal.* "Judge Told Holy Roller." December 23, 1918, 1.

into handkerchiefs and wearing sterilized gauze masks. Other suggestions sound a little less familiar, like boiling gauze masks and clothes used for handkerchiefs for thirty minutes, as well as taking medicine to open the bowels freely.[191]

The *Medina Sentinel* reported on October 25, 1918:

> *The Red Cross has samples of the gauze flu masks in the windows of the Ziegler Store, the Warner-Hemmeter Co., and DeArmitt's Department Store. These masks may be made at home, or the Red Cross will supply them on request at the abovementioned stores.*
>
> *There is no occasion for panic, but there is great necessity for every precaution. Anyone caring for the sick, or any one liable to exposure, should wear the gauze mask.*[192]

Given all of that, the Spanish flu did not dominate the business, political or social life of Medina County—or even most of the nation. The November 1918 election went on with only a few reported minor glitches. The *Columbus Dispatch* reported that an Anti-Influenza Committee in Franklin County employed a scare tactic to warn voters that they would catch the flu if they went to the polls. It was clearly a ploy by saloon interests to hinder support of the liquor prohibition issue that was on the ballot. The Anti-Saloon League forces quickly countered that voters could take reasonable precautions. They advised electors that they shouldn't put the lead pencils used to mark the ballots in their mouths, and they further suggested, "Do not spit in the voting booth. Do not cough. Do not sneeze."[193] Always good advice, I would say.

The Spanish flu was news, but it was not the only news. On the front pages of the newspapers were stories about the waning days of World War I, business activities, farming, war bond and stamp sales, Daylight Saving Time and Prohibition. Unfortunately, stories about local soldiers who died in action or from disease, as well as other notable local deaths from illness and accidents, also occupied the attention of readers.

After all of this, Medina County and the country gradually recovered from a postwar recession, the wartime costs and the Spanish flu. Political life and business prosperity soon returned, seeking a way to get back to normal. The phrase "return to normalcy" was United States presidential candidate Warren G. Harding's campaign slogan for the election of 1920. As a U.S. senator from Ohio, Harding argued, "America's present need is not heroics but healing; not nostrums but normalcy; not revolution but restoration."

SPITTING AND PROFANITY AGAINST THE LAW

Amid the Spanish flu epidemic, Medina mayor Dimmock reminded residents of a village ordinance that prohibited spitting on the sidewalks, as well as profanity in public. The *Medina Sentinel* reminded everyone, "Generally speaking, the violation of either law is equally reprehensible, but expectorating on public walks and floors is a positive menace to the physical health of the community and obviously should be stopped." In addition, the newspaper urged the mayor to follow up the warning with a few arrests of offenders. Apparently, as the newspaper pointed out the frequent posting of public signs stating, "If you spit on the floor at home, do so here, as we want you to feel at home," proved to be too subtle a reminder of proper behavior in public places to be effective.

Source: *Medina Sentinel*. "Editorial." January 3, 1919, 4.

Will that also be the next goal for many of us in a similar craving for normalcy? Perhaps, or perhaps not. I would prefer to think the progress we see in the next couple of years for Ohio will largely be based on the attributes referenced by President Harry S. Truman when he said, "America was not built on fear. America was built on courage, on imagination, and unbeatable determination to do the job at hand." No doubt, in the aftermath of COVID-19, we will have a chance to make significant changes. What they are and how our descendants view them remains to be seen.

CANCELING A MEDINA COUNTY FAIR

2020 Was Not Like 1952

*T*he year 1952 was the last time the Medina County Fair was canceled. The history books and newspaper accounts of Medina all contend it was because of the poliomyelitis (polio) epidemic. A closer look reveals that is only part of the story. According to public statements of Dr. Earl E. Kleinschmidt, the health commissioner of Medina and Wayne Counties at the time, both the closure of the fair and the concurrent closure of schools for two weeks was more in reaction to public hysteria than medical precautions.

Paralytic polio in the United States historically peaked in 1952, with 57,879 cases and 3,145 deaths—the nation's worst year on record. Ohio ranked seventh, with 3,325 cases, according to the National Foundation for Infantile Paralysis. Although it struck in both rural and urban communities throughout Ohio, Medina and Wayne Counties were among the worst hit.

At the peak of the 1952 epidemic, the 275 cases per 100,000 for Medina County made it one of the worst hit areas in the country. In July of that year, Holmes County officials enacted a quarantine and ban on large gatherings to hopefully arrest the polio outbreak. Health Commissioner Kleinschmidt disputed the effectiveness of these provisions. In a special meeting of doctors and business leaders in mid-July, he urged the public to live normally and to continue taking part in picnics, swimming, outings and every-day business. He stated, "No quarantine has ever influenced the outbreak of polio in the slightest." He followed up his advice with giving a green light to conducting the Medina County Fair in the fall. He also contended that it was public hysteria and absurd for any concerns in visiting Chippewa Lake Park or various sunshine camps located throughout the county. He advocated that the major weapon against the spread of the polio virus was, instead, strict personal cleanliness and hand washing to avoid the "hand-to-mouth danger."

Under a flood of public requests and citing a loss of $25,000, the Medina Fair Board called off the 107th annual exposition that had previously been scheduled for September 3, 1952. Shortly after that announcement, school officials throughout the county postponed the start of classes in the fall. Dr. Earl E. Kleinschmidt still refused to sanction any of these actions. Cautiously, he stated that "delaying school openings will serve no purpose scientifically, but that from the standpoint of public opinion it might be advisable."

The epidemic not only attracted a Yale University School of Medicine study of Medina and Wayne Counties, but it was fully reported in the November issue of *Public Health Reports* by the U.S. Public Health Service. Authors of the article included Dr. Kleinschmidt, Mabel Abbott of Wadsworth and E. Ilah Kauffman of Wooster. They observed in this national journal, "It has been aptly said that every poliomyelitis epidemic comprises actually two diseases, poliomyelitis and hysteria."

Jump ahead to 2020, and you have a whole new story. On June 3, the Medina Agricultural Society Board of Directors reluctantly decided to postpone the 175th Medina County Fair until 2021 because of the COVID-19 pandemic. On June 9, Governor Mike DeWine, Senate President Larry Obhof and House Speaker Larry Householder announced a new plan to reduce many of the previously issued Ohio Department of Health restrictions and provide grant money to help conduct the county fairs. Under the plan, each fair that conducted a junior fair would receive $50,000 from the state, while those that did not received $15,000 toward the following year's fair.

On June 11, after much chatter on social media, media attention and, I am certain, behind-the-scenes phone calls, the fair board rescinded the vote, and the annual exposition scheduled for August 3 through August 9 was back on. The relaxation of the prior restrictions, as well as the promised state assistance, no doubt helped that decision. Unfortunately, a second wave of COVID-19 outbreaks forced Medina officials to cancel nearly all the usual activities, except for the 4-H Junior Fair events, a week before the scheduled event.

The year 2020 was not 1952. Legitimate public health concerns were considered, and precautionary actions were taken. Borrowing from Dr. Kleinschmidt, the COVID-19 epidemic of 2020 may very well have been comprised of two diseases: COVID-19 and hysteria. The facts are, Medina

County found a way to manage both the risk of disease and curb the fears of the public. In the end, a smaller, limited but resilient 4-H Junior Medina County Fair went on in 2020. It was different from past fairs, but it was still a testament to the will and tradition of agriculture in Medina County.[194]

Epilogue

s I sit in late 2021, finishing this book, it is not easy to step aside and not mention the progress made and the ongoing challenges that Medina County residents have faced since the onset of the COVID-19 pandemic. The frequency and severity of the infectious disease has gone through some waves or cycles, and the challenges to civil discourse over masks, mandates and vaccines continues. Notwithstanding, my confidence that Medina County residents and businesses will emerge from it all stronger in the coming years remains steadfast. That will be, as I stated in the very beginning, a further restatement affirming our own collective, cherished values—the importance of families, faith, education and a democratic government. As related in the *Historic Tales of Medina County, Ohio*, these values are evident and remain immutable for our own enlightenment, if not for our posterity.

NOTES

Chapter 1

1. Alan G. Noble and Albert J. Korsok, "Ohio Physical Landscape," in *Ohio: An American Heartland*, bulletin 65 (Columbus: Ohio Department of Natural Resources, Division of Geological Survey, 1975), 4.

2. George White, "Classification of Wisconsin Glacial Deposits in Northeastern Ohio," in *Contributions to General Geology, Geological Survey Bulletin 1121-A* (Washington, D.C.: U.S. Department of the Interior, 1960), A2–A7.

3. Alfred W. Wheat, "Report on the Geology of Medina County," in *Report of the Geological Survey of Ohio*, vol. 3, part 1 (Columbus, OH: Nevins & Myers, 1878), 364.

4. J.H. Battle, Weston Arthur Goodspeed and William Henry Perrin, *History of Medina County* (Chicago: Baskins & Battey, Historical Publishers, 1881), 434–37.

5. Ibid.

6. ODNR, "History of Coal Mining in Ohio," *GeoFacts*, no. 14 (May 2005).

7. Ibid.; Wheat, "Report," 363; ODNR, "Mine Subsidence," *GeoFacts*, no. 12 (2010); "Residents Forced to Leave Wadsworth Homes Sinking Due to Possibly Collapsed Coal Mine," *Cleveland Plain Dealer*, January 11, 2019.

8. *Chatham Sesquicentennial, 1818–1968* (Chatham, OH: Chatham Sesquicentennial Committee, 1968), 18–19; Janet B. Van Doren, *Chatham, Ohio's Great Oil Adventure: A Scrapbook* (Lodi, OH: Published by Author, 2013), 1–2, 11–12, 16, 23.

9. Thomas E. Tomastik, "Large Potential Reserves Remain for Secondary Oil Recovery in Ohio," Search and Discovery Article no. 11341 (July 27, 2020), presented at the 2019 American Association of Petroleum Geologists, eastern section meeting, October 12–16, 2019, Worthington, Ohio; Van Doren, *Great Oil Adventure*, 12; "Chatham Oil Well Project Opposed," *Akron Beacon Journal*, June 2, 1987, 30; "Eastern Medina Residents, Officials Oppose Brine-Disposal Plan," *Akron Beacon Journal*, November 9, 1984, 50; Frank Munz and Phyllis Grim Siman, *The History of Chatham Township, Medina County, Ohio: Chatham Centeseptiquinarian* (Chatham, OH: Centeseptequinary Committee, 1993), 18–19; "Medina County Comprehensive Annual Financial Report, 2003," Medina County auditor, vii.

10. Wheat, "Report," 368–69; "Destination Lodi: A Historical Journey, The Vandemark Family," *Southern Medina Post Newspaper*, November 26, 2016.

Chapter 2

11. E.O. Randall and D.J. Ryan, *History of Ohio: The Rise and Progress of an American State*, vol. 3 (New York: Century History Company, 1912), 150ff; William T. Utter, *The Frontier State, 1803–1825*, vol. 2 of *The History of the State of Ohio* (Columbus: Ohio State Archaeological and Historical Society, 1942), 31.

12. J.F. Laning, "The Evolution of Ohio Counties," *Ohio Archaeological and Historical Quarterly* 5 (August 1897): 327.

13. Harlan Hatcher, *The Western Reserve: The Story of New Connecticut in Ohio* (Cleveland, OH: World Publishing Company, 1949), 49.

14. John Kilbourn, *The Ohio Gazetteer*, 9th ed. (Columbus, OH: John Kilbourn, 1829), 24.

15. Ohio secretary of state, Ohio General Assembly, *Acts of the State of Ohio, 1803*, vol. 2 (Chillicothe: Printed by N. Willis, printer to the state, 1804), 94.

16. George W. Knepper, *The Official Ohio Lands Book* (Columbus, Ohio: Auditor of State, 2002); *Atlas of Mercer County, Ohio* (Philadelphia: Griffin, Gordon & Company, 1888), 48; *Atlas and Directory of Medina County* (Cleveland, OH: American Atlas Company, 1897), 74; John Kilbourne, "The Public Lands of Ohio," in *Historical Collections: An Encyclopedia of the State*, vol. 1, ed. Henry Howe (Columbus, OH: Henry Howe & Son, 1907), 128–36.

Chapter 3

17. Jacob H. Huebert, "Judicial Elections and Their Opponents in Ohio," Federalist Society for Law & Public Policy Studies, Washington, D.C., November 2010, 1–6.

18. Ibid., 3.

19. Alfred Mathews, *Ohio and Her Western Reserve: With a Story of Three States, Leading to the Latter, From Connecticut, by Way of Wyoming, Its Indian Wares and Massacre* (New York: D. Appleton and Company, 1902), 58–60.

20. Harriet Taylor Upton, *History of the Western Reserve*, vol. 1 (New York: Lewis Publishing Company, 1910), 9–10.

21. Report of the Committee to U.S. House of Representatives of the Expediency of Accepting from the State of Connecticut a Cession of Jurisdiction of the Territory West of Pennsylvania, Commonly Called the Western Reserve of Connecticut, March 21, 1800, 25.

22. Ellen D. Larned, "New Connecticut or Western Reserve," *Connecticut Quarterly* 2, no. 4 (October, November, December 1896): 386–95.

23. Ibid.; *Report of the Committee*, 25, 31; Beverley W. Bond Jr., *The Foundations of Ohio: A History of the State of Ohio*, ed. Carl Wittke, vol. 1 (Columbus: Ohio Historical Society, 1941), 454–55; Upton, *Western Reserve*, 1:9–10; Henry Howe, *Historical Collections of Ohio* (Cincinnati, OH: Bradley and Anthony, 1850), 12.

24. Upton, *Western Reserve*, 1:20.

25. Ibid., 22–23; James Harrison Kennedy, *A History of the City of Cleveland: Its Settlement, Rise and Progress, 1796–1896* (Cleveland, OH: Imperial Press, 1896), 32; George E. Condon, *Cleveland: Prodigy of the Western Reserve* (Tulsa, OK: Continental Heritage Press, 1979), 20–21.

26. Annals of Congress, House of Representatives, 6th Congress, 1st session, 662–63, 658; Journal of the Senate of the United States of America, 1789–1873, April 23, 1800.

27. Utter, *Frontier State*, 3–31.

Chapter 4

28. Charles B. Galbreath, *History of Ohio*, vol. 2 (Chicago: American Historical Society Inc., 1925), 286.

Chapter 5

29. New England Historical Society, "1816: The Year Without a Summer," www.newenglandhistoricalsociety.com; Michael Munger, "1816: The Mighty Operations of Nature: An Environmental History of the Year Without a Summer," (master's thesis, University of Oregon, June 2012); William K. Klingaman and Nicholas P. Klingaman, "Tambora Erupts in 1815 and Changes World History," *Scientific American Magazine*, March 1, 2013.

30. "Reports from the *Albany Gazette* and Portland, Maine," *Hartford Courant*, October 15, 1816, 2.

31. "Domestic Economy," *American Yeoman* (Brattleboro, VT) April 8, 1817, 4, reprinted from the *Hampshire Gazette*.

32. Mathews, *Ohio and Her Western Reserve*, 24.

33. Ibid., 33.

34. N.B. Northrup, *Pioneer History of Medina County* (Medina, OH: George Redway, 1861), 136.

Chapter 6

35. Marjorie E. Kornhauser, "Taxing Bachelors in America: 1895–1939," Tulane Public Law Research Paper no. 17-7, July 12, 2012, 1, 4–11, 27–28.

36. "Freak Legislation," *Medina Sentinel*, April 16, 1915, 4.

37. "Legislatures of Many States are Considering Bills Planned to Tax the Carefree Bachelor Out of Existence," *Baltimore Sun*, March 7, 1909, 1.

38. "State Press Comment," *Courier-Post* (Camden, NJ), February 13, 1903, 4; "Woman on Racial Suicide," *Baltimore Sun* (Baltimore, MD), February 23, 1903, 7; "President Roosevelt Is Given Rousing Welcome By Citizens and School Children of Oakland," *San Francisco Call* (San Francisco, CA), May 15, 1903, 6; "No Race Suicide in South," *Times-Democrat* (New Orleans, LA), September 16, 1903, 6; "Criticized Jefferson," *Brunswick Daily News*, September 1, 1903, 2; "Life of Roosevelt," *Ogden Standard*, May 29, 1903, 7.

39. "There's a Club for Everything," *Hartford City Telegram* (Hartford City, IN), July 5, 1904, 4.

40. "Taxing Bachelors," *Monmouth Daily Atlas* (Monmouth, IL) April 13, 1921, 6.

41. J.H. Galbreath, "Short Stories of the Buckeye State: A Bachelor Tax in Ohio," *Columbus Evening Dispatch*, July 6, 1918, 4.

42. Ohio Constitutional Convention, 1912, proceedings and debates, April 1, 1912, 979.

43. "No Bachelor Tax," *Columbus Evening Dispatch*, March 29, 1912, 16.

44. Ohio Constitutional Convention, 1912, proceedings and debates, March 25, 1912, 868; "Henry Eby," *Defiance Daily Crescent News*, March 25, 1912, 9.

45. "Theodore Herbert is Dead," *San Francisco Call*, May 15, 1911, 5; "Women Workers Guests in Bachelors Hotel," *San Francisco Examiner*, December 22, 1912, 10; "Places," *San Francisco Examiner*, October 5, 1975, 282; "Bachelors Hotel Invaded," *San Francisco Call*, July 23, 1913, 1; "Noted Hotel Keeper Comes to Los Gatos," *Los Gatos Star* (Los Gatos, CA) August 15, 1929, 4.

46. "A Price on American Heiresses," *Ogden Standard*, August 8, 1914, 19; "Stanley Bowdle Killed by Auto Near His Home," *Cincinnati Commercial Tribune*, April 7, 1919, 1.

47. Kornhauser, "Taxing Bachelors," 28–29.

Chapter 7

48. "End Is Near for Seville's House of Giants," *Akron Beacon Journal*, April 12, 1948, 15.

49. "The Giants Wedding," *New York-Daily Tribune*, July 1, 1871; Bates, Martin Van Buren marriage license, no. 449, Parish of the St. Martin in the Field, 1871; "Giants' Wedding," *Bristol Mercury and Daily Post*, June 24, 1871, 3; "A Remarkable Marriage," *Freeman's Journal* (Dublin, Ireland) June 24, 1871, 6; "Will of Capt. Bates Filed for Probate," *Medina Sentinel*, December 5, 1919, 1.

50. *Captain Bates Autobiography* (1880), as cited by William P. Thayer, James McCauley and Karen McCauley, "Captain Bates Autobiography," 2009, www.yeahpot.com; "A Giant," *Wyandot Pioneer* (Upper Sandusky, OH), August 2, 1865, 1; "A Giant," *Cincinnati Daily Commercial*, July 17, 1865, 5.

51. Prisoner of War Source Citation—Camp Chase, Ohio, National Archives, Washington, D.C.; War Department Collection of Confederate Records, NARA film publication no. M598, record group: War Department Collection of Confederate Records, record group no. 109; U.S. Civil War Prisoner of War Records (Camp Chase), 1861–1865 for Martin V. Bates, microfilm 28,970, 22,946.

52. Ohio History Connection, "Ohio History Central: Camp Chase," www. ohiohistorycentral.org; William H. Knauss, *The Story of Camp Chase: A History of the Prison and Its Cemetery, Together with Other Cemeteries Where Confederate Prisoners are Buried, etc.* (Nashville, TN: Publishing House of the Methodist Episcopal Church, South Smith & Lamar, agents, 1906), 128, 139; "Political Prisoners at Camp Chase," *Daily Statesman* (Columbus, OH), November 29, 1862, 2; Martin Kelly, "Civil War Prisoner Exchange: Changing Rules Concerning Prisoner Exchange During the Civil War," ThoughtCo., March 6, 2017, www.thoughtco.com.

53. Arthur Dixon, "The Giant of the Hills: Martin Van Buren Bates," *First National Bank Chronicles*, September 6, 2008, 5, reprint from *Independent Herald*, August 5, 1993.

54. Thayer, McCauley and McCauley, "Autobiography"; "The Life History of Seville Giant and Giantess Recalled by Autobiography," *Medina County Gazette*, July 23, 1937, 3, 7; Grace Goulder, "Ohio Songs and Citizens: They Recall When Giants Lived Among Them," *Cleveland Plain Dealer Pictorial Magazine*, February 20, 1944, 15.

55. "Marriage in 'High' Life," *Highland Weekly News*, July 27, 1871, 4; "A Giant," *Cincinnati Daily Commercial*, July 17, 1865, 5; "A Giant," *Wyandot Pioneer* (Upper Sandusky, OH), August 2, 1865, 1, reprint from the *Louisville Journal*, July 12, 1865.

56. "A Giantess Dead," *Hornellsville Weekly Tribune*, September 7, 1888, 1; Joyce Crislip, *The First Baptist Church of Seville, Ohio: 175 Years of Church History Consolidated from Several Documents* (Seville, OH: First Baptist Church, 2013).

57. "Spanish Influenza," *New Castle Herald*, October 5, 1918, 4.

58. "Seville's History Filled with Colorful Memories," *Medina County Gazette*, February 24, 1967, 5; "After Anna's Death: Martin Van Buren Bates and Annette Lavonne Weatherby," Annette Potter Family Genealogy, www. yeahpot.com; Joann G. King, *Medina County Coming of Age, 1810–1900* (Cleveland, OH: Angstrom Graphics, 2016), 345–52.

59. Martin Van Buren Bates death certificate, State of Ohio, Bureau of Vital Statistics, January 10, 1919, cited by Patty May Brashear, "Martin Van Buren Bates: The Kentucky River Giant, Part II," www.wright-bates.com; "World's Tallest Man, Once Circus Attraction, Dead," *Akron Evening Times*, January 13, 1919, 1; "Death of Famous Giant, MV Bates at Seville," *Medina Sentinel*, January 10, 1919, 1; "The Passing of Captain Gates," *Medina Gazette*, January 17, 1919, 1; "Capt. M.V. Bates, Noted Giant, and His Widow," *Medina Sentinel*, January 17, 1919, 1; "Bates Dies on Tuesday," *Medina Gazette*, April 5, 1940, 1.

60. "Natural Selection," *Sheffield and Rotherham Independent* (Sheffield, UK) June 20, 1871, 6; "Giants in These Days," *Athens Messenger*, February 16, 1882, 6; "Several Famous Giants," *Brooklyn Times*, June 8, 1889, 1, 4.
61. "Pioneers in Human Development," *Times-Picayune*, June 2, 1878, 4.
62. Michael J. Dougherty, "Why are We Getting Taller as a Species?" *Scientific American*, June 29, 1998, www.scientificamerican.com; Philip B. Kunhardt Jr., Philip B. Kunhardt III and Peter W. Kunhardt, *P.T. Barnum: America's Greatest Showman* (New York: Alfred A. Knopf, 1995), 175, 235.

Chapter 8

63. Randell and Ryan, *History of Ohio*, 4:483.
64. *Biographical Cyclopedia and Portrait Gallery with an Historical Sketch of the State of Ohio*, vol. 1 (Cincinnati, OH: Western Biographical Publishing Company, 1883), 180–83; "Death Summons Governor Nash," *Marion Star*, October 28, 1904, 1.
65. "Seals and Ohio Flag," *Bulletin of the Ohio State Library* 3, 181–83; John M. Purcell FFIAV, "The Centennial of Ohio's Flag: From Obscurity to Esteem," *19th International Congress of Vexillology*, 2001, 181–84; Ohio House of Representatives, *Ohio House Journal*, May 8, 1902, 445.

Chapter 9

66. "General Harris Takes Oath," *Democrat-Sentinel* (Logan, OH), June 21, 1906, 1.
67. "Former Governor Andrew L. Harris Passes Away at Home in Eaton," *Dayton Daily News*, September 13, 1915, 1, 11.
68. "Warrior and Statesman, Too; Colonel Andrew L. Harris, New Governor of Ohio," *Cincinnati Enquirer*, June 19, 1906, 2; "Gov. Anderson: Death of One of Ohio's Most Distinguished Sons," *Cincinnati Enquirer*, September 3, 1895, 1; "Stories of Ohio: Governor Charles Anderson," *Dayton Daily News*, August 3, 1927, 10; "Ohio's Governors," *Cincinnati Enquirer*, April 29, 1879, 5; "Ohio Governors: Charles Anderson," *Dayton Daily News*, February 24, 1946, 15; Randell and Ryan, *History of Ohio*, 4:458–60.
69. "General Harris Takes Oath," *Democrat-Sentinel* (Logan, OH), June 21, 1906, 1; "Governor Will Not Call Extra Session," *Chronicle-Telegram* (Elyria, OH), June 23, 1906, 1,8; "Governor Harris Is Governor," *Akron*

Beacon Journal, June 19, 1906, 1; "General Harris Takes the Oath," *Marysville Journal-Tribune* (Marysville, OH), June 19, 1906, 1; "Amazed by Their Audacity," *Cincinnati Enquirer* (Cincinnati, OH), June 24, 1906, 3; "Andrew Harris, Governor," *Union County Journal* (Marysville, OH), July 26, 1906, 4.

70. "Ruling by Ellis on Wet and Dry," *Evening Review* (East Liverpool, OH), June 25, 1908, 1; "The Chances for County Local Option," *Sandusky Star-Journal* (Sandusky, OH), January 3, 1908, 4.

71. Galbreath, *History of Ohio*, 2:688–89.

72. "Rose Bill Has Hoodoo '23,'" *Dayton Herald*, March 7, 1908, 2.

73. "Medina County's Vote," *Medina County Gazette*, November 4, 1908, 4.

74. "Taft Speaks to Thousands," *Daily Reflector* (Norwalk, OH), October 14, 1908, 1; "Swinging Through Country Taft Is Met by Throngs," *Akron Beacon Journal*, October 13, 1908, 1; "Presidential Candidate Taft Gets Magnificent Welcome," *Akron Beacon Journal*, October 13, 1908, 1.

75. "Election Results: The Pluralities," *Akron Beacon Journal*, November 7, 1908, 4; "Medina County Vote," *Medina County Gazette*, November 4, 1908, 4.

76. "Medina County Vote," *Medina County Gazette*, November 4, 1908, 4.

77. "Double Dealing of Governor Harris," *Daily Crescent News* (Defiance, OH), October 14, 1908, 4.

78. "Battle of the Ballots Today," *Evening Review* (East Liverpool, OH), November 3, 1908, 7.

79. James K. Mercer, *Ohio Legislative History: 1909–1912*, vol. 1 (Columbus, OH: Edward T. Miller Co.), 16; Randell and Ryan, *History of Ohio*, 4:462.

Chapter 10

80. Randell and Ryan, *History of Ohio*, 3:125.

81. "Ohio Election Returns—Official," *Democratic Sentinel and Harrison County Farmer*, July 16, 1851, 2.

82. "GM Titus of Muscatine Talks for Biennial Elections at Convention of County Officers," *Muscatine Journal* (Muscatine, IA), August 19, 1904, 2; Galbreath, *History of Ohio*, 2:682.

83. "Too Many Elections," *Cleveland Plain Dealer*, September 17, 1886, 4; Galbreath, *History of Ohio*, 2:682.

84. Galbreath, *History of Ohio*, 2:79; "The Election." *Medina County Gazette*, August 21, 1874, 2.

85. "Biennial Elections," *Columbus Evening Dispatch*, December 18, 1888, 1; "This Settles It: The Biennial Elections Amendment Was Not Adopted," *Cleveland Plain Dealer*, December 18, 1889, 2; "The Biennial Election Amendment Not Adopted," *Dayton Herald*, December 17, 1889, 2; "A Suggestion," *Lima Clipper*, December 1, 1889, 1.

86. Isaac Franklin Patterson, "State and County Elections in Even Years Amendment, 1905," in *The Constitutions of Ohio: Amendments ad Proposed Amendments* (Cleveland, OH: Artur H. Clark Company, 1912), 288–90; "Terms of Officials Will Be Extended in Ohio: Biennial Election Amendment Creates a Chaotic Condition of Affairs in this State—Present Officials Will Profit by It," *Akron Beacon Journal*, November 23, 1905, 2; "Official Vote," *Medina Sentinel*, November 10, 1905, 4.

87. "Another Year of Herrick," *Cleveland Plain Dealer*, November 11, 1905, 1.

88. "Fewer Elections," *Cleveland Plain Dealer*, November 13, 1885, 4; "Biennial Elections," *Columbus Evening Dispatch*; "Double Liability: Senate Votes Unanimously to Do Away With It—Proposition to Abolish Annual Election—To Cure Pass Evil," *Columbus Evening Dispatch*, February 20, 1902, 5; "Needs Legislation," *Columbus Evening Dispatch*, November 13, 1905, 2; "Governor-Elect Will Have Term of Three Years," *Columbus Evening Dispatch*, November 8, 1905, 2; "Biennial Sessions," *Columbus Evening Dispatch*, January 1896, 11; "Hold Biennial Elections," *Cleveland Plain Dealer*, February 24, 1904, 1.

89. Raymond L. Bridgman, *Biennial Elections* (Boston: D.C. Heath and Company, 1896), 146.

90. "GM Titus of Muscatine Talks For Biennial Elections at Convention of County Officers in Dubuque," *Muscatine Journal* (Muscatine, IA), August 19, 1904, 2.

Chapter 11

91. Proceedings and Debates: Ohio Constitutional Convention, vol. 2, April 16, 1912, 1,231.

92. Proceedings and Debates: Ohio Constitutional Convention, May 1, 1912, 1,522.

Chapter 12

93. Upton, *Western Reserve*, 1:382; Battle, Goodspeed and Perrin, *Medina County*, 420.

94. Upton, *Western Reserve*, 1:383.

95. Battle, Goodspeed and Perrin, *Medina County*, 301; J.E. Hagerty, C.P. McClelland and C.C. Huntington, *History of the Ohio Canals: Their Construction, Cost, Use and Partial Abandonment* (Columbus: Ohio State Archeological and Historical Society, 1905), 127–32; Harold E. Davis, "Economic Basis for Ohio Politics, 1820–1840," *Ohio History Journal* 47, no. 4 (October 1938): 301–5; Stephen D. Hambley, *Timeline of Medina County History* (Brunswick, OH: Self-published, 2018), 8.

96. "Wadsworth Is Now Knocking at Our Doors," *Akron Beacon Journal*, February 21, 1911, 1.

97. Stephen D. Hambley, "The Vanguard of a Regional Infrastructure: Electric Railways of Northeast Ohio, 1884–1932" (PhD diss., University of Akron, 1993).

98. "Wadsworth Is in Favor of This County," *Akron Beacon Journal*, January 16, 1912, 1; "Wadsworth Complaining," *Medina Sentinel*, January 19, 1912, 5.

99. "Akron Merchants Want Wadsworth," *Akron Beacon Journal*, February 22, 1911, 1; "Wadsworth Summit County?" *Orrville Courier*, February 24, 1911, 1; "Wadsworth Is Now Knocking at Our Doors," *Akron Beacon Journal*, February 21, 1911, 1.

100. Poor's Manual Company, *Poor's Manual of Railroads* (New York: Poor's Manual Company, 1907), 1,264–65; "Wadsworth," Akron Beacon Journal, May 4, 1907, 13; "Cannon Boomed, Whistles Blew and the Band Played," *Akron Beacon Journal*, April 9, 1907, 12; Hambley, "Vanguard of a Regional Infrastructure."

101. "Claims Wets Are Behind Annexation," *Akron Beacon Journal*, February 23, 1911.

102. "How It Happened That Wadsworth Went 'Wet,'" *Akron Times-Democrat*, August 7, 1902, 7.

103. "Wadsworth and Medina Co. Dry," *Akron Beacon Journal*, December 16, 1908.

104. "Chamber of Commerce Scores Great Victory," *Akron Beacon Journal*, May 1, 1912.

105. Proceedings and Debates of the Constitutional Convention of Ohio, February 26, 1912, 450–56.

106. "Vote on Three Amendments," *Mahoning Dispatch*, September 6, 1912, 8.

107. "Five Initiative Petitions to be Served On Legislature," *Akron Beacon Journal*, December 27, 1912, 9.

108. "Vote Town Dry in Wadsworth," *Medina Sentinel*, December 4, 1914, 1.

109. "Wadsworth Votes Dry," *Salem News*, December 16, 1914, 6.

Chapter 13

110. "Automotive History: Cleveland was Almost the Motor City," *Smart Business*, May 1, 2013; "Automotive Industry," David D. Van Tassel and John J. Grabowski, eds., *The Encyclopedia of Cleveland History* (Indianapolis: Indiana University Press, 1987), 57–58.

111. *Atlas and Directory of Medina*, 55.

112. "An $80,000 Inn in a Town of 800 People," *Cleveland Sunday Plain Dealer*, March 19, 1905, 5.

113. Mapes, "Taylor Inn."

114. Lodi Harrisville Historical Society, "Destination Lodi, A Historical Journey, The Taylor Inn, Part 2," www.lodiharrisvillehistorical.org; Mapes, "Taylor Inn"; *Atlas and Directory of Medina*, 55; Medina County Historical Society, *History of Medina County* (Fostoria, OH: Gray Printing Company, 1948), 122.

115. "Society News—Lodi," *Cleveland Plain Dealer*, October 11, 1903, 7; Van Tassel and Grabowski, *Encyclopedia*, 515; "Lyman-Bishop: Marriage of a Medina Young Lady and an Akron Business Man," *Medina Sentinel*, October 2, 1903, 5; "The Full Measure of Success," *Cleveland Plain Dealer*, May 27, 1903, 6.

116. Van Tassel and Grabowski, *Encyclopedia*, 736; H. Roger Grant, *Ohio on the Move: Transportation in the Buckeye State* (Athens: Ohio University Press, 2000), 11–12; James Flink, *America Adopts the Automobile, 1895–1910* (Cambridge, MA: MIT Press, 1970), 45, 144–63; "Sing Praises of the Automobile," *Cleveland Plain Dealer*, April 28, 1903, 4.

117. "Finished Pleasant Run," *Cleveland Plain Dealer*, May 25, 1903, 10.

118. "Inn Is Saved from Sheriff," *Medina County Gazette*, April 27, 1937, 1, 4; Mapes, "Taylor Inn"; "Halts Destruction," *Medina County Gazette*, June 29, 1937, 1; "Brief Items of Interest," *Medina County Gazette*, February 15, 1938, 1.

Chapter 14

119. "Woman Suffrage," *Wellington Enterprise*, March 13, 1895, 8.

120. "Pledge to Aid New Voters," *Cincinnati Enquirer*, August 19, 1920, 14.

121. "Election Results," *Medina Sentinel*, November 7, 1913, 1.

122. "Ohio Women Get Presidential Suffrage Soon," *Medina Sentinel*, August 29, 1919, 6; "Women Will Not Vote in April," *Lima News*, April 17, 1920, 1.

123. "Not Subject to Referendum," *Lancaster Eagle-Gazette*, June 2, 1920, 1.

Chapter 15

124. "Walter Fenton Laid to Rest," *Medina Sentinel*, August 24, 1944, 1; "In 100th Year: Cora Blakeslee Operated Hardware Store 25 Years," *Medina County Gazette*, May 18, 1956, 6; "Medina County and Its People: Albert Munson and Daughter Cora," *Medina County Gazette*, September 28, 1956, 2, 8; "Additional County Notes," *Medina Gazette*, August 29, 1879, 5; "Equal Woman's Suffrage," *Medina Sentinel*, October 16, 1914, 8; "Former Merchant Still Going Strong: Mrs. Blakeslee," Medina County Gazette, February 12, 1954, 1, 5.

125. "Election Results: How Medina Voted," *Medina Sentinel*, September 6, 1912, 1.

126. "Vote on Amendments," *Medina Sentinel*, November 9, 1917, 1; "Wet Majority in Ohio 1,137 Votes," *Medina Sentinel*, November 23, 1917, 11.

Chapter 17

127. "How Will the Soldiers Vote," *Perrysburg Journal* (Perrysburg, OH), July 17, 1868, 1; "The Soldiers Right to Vote," *Delaware Gazette* (Delaware, OH), September 20, 1867, 1.

128. Randell and Ryan, *History of Ohio*, 4:228–38; Eugene H. Roseboom, *The History of the State of Ohio: The Civil War Era, 1850–1873* (Columbus, OH: Ohio State Archeological and Historical Society, 1944), 421–23; Galbreath, *History of Ohio*, 2:570–75; "Vote of Ohio Volunteers," *Civilian and Telegraph* (Cumberland, MD), October 15, 1863, 2; "John Brough for Governor," *Cleveland Daily Leader*, June 15, 1863, 2; "Union State Ticket," *Jeffersonian Democrat* (Chardon, OH), June 26, 1863, 2; "The Two Democracies," *Lancaster Gazette* (Lancaster, OH), September 24, 1863, 2; "The Ohio Election," *Cincinnati Daily Commercial*, October 15, 1863 3;

"Union State Ticket," *Washington Fayette County Herald*, October 8, 1863, 5; John Patterson Smith, *History of the Republican Party in Ohio*, vol. 1 (Chicago: Lewis Publishing Company, 1898), 160–62.

129. Smith, *History of the Republican Party*, 1:153–62.

130. Galbreath, *History of Ohio*, 2:572; "Democratic Slate Ticket," *Cambridge Guernsey Jeffersonian*, September 25, 1863, 3; "Democratic State Nominations," *Defiance Democrat*, August 1, 1863, 2; "Ohio Democratic State Convention," *Cincinnati Daily Commercial*, June 12, 1863, 2; "Journalists of Logan County," *Stewart's Combination Atlas Map of Logan County 1875*, vol. 12 (Philadelphia, PA: N.p., 1875); *History of Logan County* (Chicago: O.L. Baskin & Co., 1880), 283; "Treasurer of State," *Ashland Union*, May 27, 1857, 2; Roseboom, *History of the State of Ohio*, 4:421–23.

131. "Notice of Contest," *Freemont Weekly Journal*, November 6, 1863, 2; "The Soldiers Right to Vote: Who Opposed it? Who Favored It?" *Delaware Gazette*, September 20, 1867, 1; "For the Pioneer: Letter to the Editor," *Wyandot Pioneer* (Upper Sandusky, OH), November 27, 1863, 3; "The Army Vote," *Cambridge Guernsey Jeffersonian*, December 4, 1863, 1.

132. William T. Patterson, "Letter from the 116th OVI, Martinsburg, VA, September 26, 1863," *Athens Messenger* 20, no. 41 (October 15, 1863): 1.

133. "More of the Private Talk of the Soldiers," *Cincinnati Enquirer*, March 13, 1863, 2.

134. "Ohio Results," *Civilian and Telegraph* (Cumberland, MD) October 15, 1863, 2; "The Vote Given for Democratic and Republican Governors for the Last Ten Years—Gigantic Frauds Perpetrated," *Cincinnati Enquirer*, October 26, 1863, 2; "Bill to Allow Soldiers to Vote," *Cleveland Daily Leader*, February 2, 1863, 2.

135. "A Military Election Farce," quoting the *Fort Wayne Sentinel*, *Cincinnati Enquirer*, November 12, 1863, 1.

136. "From the 107th Regiment: The Democratic Soldiers Not Permitted to Vote," *Ashland Union*, November 18, 1863, 1.

137. "The Soldier Vote in Ohio," *Cincinnati Enquirer*, November 17, 1863, 2.

138. "Ashland County Copperheadism," *Western Reserve Chronicle* (Warren, OH) November 25, 1853, 2; "The Election Contest," *Ashland Union*, December 16, 1863, 2; "Notice," *Fremont Weekly Journal*, 2; "Copperheads Opposing the Soldiers Vote," *Lancaster Gazette*, December 31, 1863, 2; "Columbus Correspondence," *Cleveland Plain Dealer*, January 23, 1864, 2.

139. Smith, *History of the Republican Party*, 1:162; "A Correct Official Vote," *Cincinnati Enquirer*, December 29, 1863, 3; "Abraham Lincoln," *Chicago*

Tribune, January 13, 1885, 9; George W. Knepper, *Ohio and Its People* (Kent, OH: Kent State University Press, 1989), 245.

140. "The Postal Ballot," *Coshocton Tribune,* June 4, 1914, 4.

141. "Voting by Mail," *Medina Sentinel,* December 19, 1919, 10.

142. "Governor Address: State Expenses Much Too Great," *Marion Star,* January 12, 1915, 11; Galbreath, *History of Ohio,* 2:711–12.

143. "Confidence," *Cincinnati Enquirer,* October 25, 1924, 4.

144. "Getting Out the Vote Fever Becomes Mania as New Plans are Made," *Dayton Daily News,* September 23, 1923, 7; "Voting by Mail," *Sandusky Star Journal,* November 2, 1920, 12; "Absent Voters Were Busy at University," *Athens Messenger,* October 26, 1920, 5.

145. "Voting By Mail," *Akron Evening Times,* September 18, 1919, 6.

Chapter 20

146. "Political Advertisement: Fremont E. Tanner," *Medina Sentinel,* November 2, 1921, 5, 7; "Political Advertisement: Fremont E. Tanner," *Medina Sentinel,* August 3, 1922, 3.

147. "Donahey and Thompson Both Win," *Medina Sentinel,* August 10, 1922, 1.

148. "Smith Decides Election Contest," *Circleville Daily Union Herald,* August 26, 1922, 1; "Tanner to Be Opposed," *Columbus Sunday Dispatch,* August 20, 1922, 17; "Thirty Years Ago: 1923," *Medina County Gazette,* January 30, 1953, 10; "Announcements," *Defiance Crescent News,* January 30, 1923, 8; "Fremont E. Tanner Now County Surveyor," *Medina Sentinel,* January 25, 1923, 1.

149. *Medina County Commissioners Journal* 14 (April 23, 1923): 95; "Formally Ask Tanner to Quit," *Medina Sentinel,* April 25, 1923, 1; "Prosecutor in Role of Mediator," *Medina Sentinel,* May 3, 1923, 1.

150. *Medina County Commissioners Journal* 14 (May 29, 1924): 345; "Notes," *Kent Tribune,* October 9, 1924, 4; "Tanner Petitions Court for Order," *Medina Sentinel,* February 26, 1925, 1, 6; "Jail Knocked by Grand Jury," *Medina Sentinel,* January 8, 1925, 1; "F.E. Tanner and Editor Baldwin Charge Each Other with Assault," *Medina Sentinel,* October 2, 1924, 1, 6; "Surveyor Tanner's Weekly Report," *Medina Sentinel,* March 15, 1923, 1; *Board of Medina County Commissioners Journal,* September 30, 1924, 426; "Park Board Wins Action," *Cincinnati Enquirer,* December 30, 1925, 8; "Medina," *Elyria Chronicle Telegram,* March 24, 1924, 11.

151. "Assault Case Against Tanner to Be Nolled," *Medina Sentinel*, September 10, 1925, 1; "Ex-Surveyor Dies," *Medina County Gazette*, June 29, 1954, 1.

Chapter 21

152. "Camp Avery: A Forgotten Outpost in Northern Ohio," *Lake Erie Ledger*, Publication of the Society of the War of 1812, July 2006, 309.
153. Grant, *Ohio on the Move*, 21.
154. "Forms Organization," *Medina County Gazette*, January 27, 1939, 1; "Road Group Meets to Elect Officers," *Akron Beacon Journal*, January 6, 1941, 15.
155. "State to Open Route 18 Bids," *Medina County Gazette*, November 17, 1939, 1.
156. "Route 18 on Approved List," *Medina County Gazette*, December 27, 1938, 1.
157. "Formal Opening of Medina Road Celebrated," *Akron Beacon Journal*, December 6, 1941, 9.
158. Ibid., 1; "Medina Has Big Part in Route 18 Opening Friday," *Medina County Gazette*, December 9, 1941, 1.
159. "Medina Has Big Part in Route 18 Opening Friday," *Medina County Gazette*, December 9, 1941, 1.
160. "Early Motoring Days on Route 18 Were Thus," *Medina County Gazette*, December 5, 1941, 1.
161. "Medina Has Big Part in Route 18 Opening Friday," *Medina County Gazette*, December 9, 1941, 1.
162. "ODOT 2006–2001 Major New Construction Program List," Tier 1—Projects for Construction SFYs 2006–2011, May 12, 2005; "Major Area Road Projects," *Akron Beacon Journal*, March 18, 2004, A9; "Route 18 Finally Get Its Face-Lift," *Akron Beacon Journal*, July 23, 2006, B1, B7.
163. "Route 18 Finally," *Akron Beacon Journal*, B, B7.

Chapter 22

164. "Feudin' Farmers Continue Battle in Medina County," *Marion Star*, January 19, 1939, 1; "Shaffer Promises Hog Farm Will Be in 'Best Condition,'" *Akron Beacon Journal*, March 30, 1939, 27; "Hog Farm Nuisance?" *Cincinnati Enquirer*, February 4, 1939, 15; "Feeding Garbage to

Hogs Starts Controversy," *Chicago Tribune*, January 19, 1939, 1; "Pig Garbage Case Showdown Coming," *Washington C.H. Record-Herald*, February 3, 1939, 1; "Sign Calls Medina 'Dump Ground' for Cuyahoga Garbage," *News-Journal*, January 19, 1939, 1; "Newspaper Takes Up Garbage Fight," *Daily Times* (New Philadelphia, OH), January 25, 1939, 7.

165. "Kievet Is Silent on Ouster Charge," *Akron Beacon Journal*, May 29, 1939, 9; "'Pig Farm' Ruled Menace to Health," *Wilmington News Journal*, June 8, 1939, 1; "Bedford Wins Hog Farm Suit; Harper Loses Out," *Medina County Gazette*, August 18, 1939, 1.

166. "County Health Board Must Rule One Way or Other—Freiberg in Controversy," *Cincinnati Enquirer*, February 4, 1939, 15; "Eyssen Attacks Health Board," *Medina County Gazette*, April 4, 1939, 1; Harry F. Gray, president of the International Piston Ring Company of Cleveland and charter member of the American Legion Post in Brunswick, wrote at least two letters to the editor very critical of both. (*Medina County Gazette*, January 24, 1939, and *Medina County Gazette*, March 7, 1939, 2.) The Gray family were longtime residents of Brunswick in the Strongs Corners area (Sleepy Hollow Lake Road and Pearl Road)—about three miles south of the offending odorous pig farm—but not close enough to be considered a "not in my back yard" (NIMBY) kind of concern. Harry F. Gray was joined by R.T. Elliott of Hinckley and Floyd Bennett of Medina in complaining about other garbage-fed pig operations in Medina County ("Letter to the Editor: Public Health Menace," *Akron Beacon Journal*, April 4, 1939, 4).

167. "Republican Voters Spurn Third Terms," *Medina County Gazette*, May 17, 1940, 1; "William G. Bacthelder Jr. Political Advertisement," *Medina County Gazette*, May 3, 1940, 4; "Unofficial Republic Primary Results," *Medina County Gazette*, May 17, 1940, 8.

168. "William G. Batchelder Jr. Obituary," *Akron Beacon Journal*, May 11, 2011, B004.

169. "Akron May Face Garbage Problem," *Akron Beacon Journal*, January 20, 1939, 1.

Chapter 23

170. "For Colored Margarine," *Akron Beacon Journal*, November 1, 1949, 6; "Proposed Law," *Akron Beacon Journal*, November 7, 1949, 6.

171. "Cherished Privilege," *Medina County Gazette*, November 9, 1949, 2; "All Levies Are Approved in Election," *Medina County Gazette*, November 11,

1949, 1, 3; "State Issue History," compiled through 1954 by Arthur A. Schwartz, director, Legislative Reference Bureau, maintained through present by the Office of the Ohio Secretary of State.

172. Rebecca Rupp, "The Butter Wars: When Margarine Was Pink," *National Geographic*, August 13, 2014, www.nationalgeographic.com; Adam Young, "The War on Margarine: The Dairy Lobby Employed Many Weapons in Its Long Fight," *Foundation for Economic Education*, June 2002; Richard A. Ball and J. Robert Lilly, "The Menace of Margarine: The Rise and Fall of a Social Problem," *Social Problems* 29, no. 5 (June 1982): 488–98; Ruth Dupré, "'If It's Yellow, It Must Be Butter': Margarine Regulation in North America Since 1886," *Journal of Economic History* 59, no. 2 (1999): 353–71, www.jstor.org.

Chapter 24

173. "410-House Project Ahead in Brunswick," *Cleveland Plain Dealer*, November 29, 1955, 31; Franklin Brothers advertisement, *Cleveland Plain Dealer*, July 7, 1957, 77; "Table 920, Hours and Gross Earning of Production Workers in Manufacturing, 1950 to 1958," in *1959 Statistical Abstract of the United States*, 80th ed. (Washington, D.C.: U.S. Department of Commerce, Bureau of Census, 1959), 231; "Builders Tell Why: New Housing Cost Here is 2nd Highest," *Akron Beacon Journal*, June 27, 1959, 15.

174. "410-House Project Ahead in Brunswick," *Cleveland Plain Dealer*, November 29, 1955, 31.

175. "Tri-County Plan Board," *Akron Beacon Journal*, November 18, 1959, 39.

176. "Township to Vote on Status," *Akron Beacon Journal*, February 21, 1958, 24; "Want to Secede," *Akron Beacon Journal*, December 2, 1959, 30; "Second Brunswick Secession Looms," *Akron Beacon Journal*, March 25, 1960, 8; "Will Ballot April 26 on Secession," *Akron Beacon Journal*, April 13, 1960, 9; "Second Village May Form in Brunswick Hills Township," *Akron Beacon Journal*, June 24, 1960, 4; Sam Boyer, "Resistance Gave Birth to Brunswick Hills Township: Brunswick at 50," *Brunswick Sun News*, October 3, 2010, www.brunswickhistory.com.

177. "A Look at 'Fiery' Brunswick," *Akron Beacon Journal*, October 19, 1960, 1, 2; "Court Dismisses Move to Block Brunswick Twp," *Akron Beacon Journal*, March 5, 1960, 2.

178. "Brunswick Must Find Water," *Akron Beacon Journal*, October 11, 1960, 8.

179. "Brunswick to Obtain Its Water," *Akron Beacon Journal*, November 7, 1962, 7; "As Bond Issue Wins," *Akron Beacon Journal*, November 8, 1962, 71; "Brunswick Group Backs Water Bonds, *Akron Beacon Journal*, October 31, 1962, 80.

180. "Medina Water Project Foes Charge 'Fraud' by County," *Akron Beacon Journal*, August 17, 1976, 4; "Brunswick Trustees Cry 'Betrayal in Water Fight," *Akron Beacon Journal*, April 26, 1977, 6.

Chapter 25

181. Root, "Wright Brothers Story," www.rootcandles.com; "Wright Brothers' Flying Machine: The First Reporter," *NOVA* PBS series, created in 2003, www.pbs.org; "Our Homes by Al Root," *Gleanings in Bee Culture* 32, no. 5 (March 1, 1904): 241–42; "Our Homes by Al Root," *Gleanings in Bee Culture* 33, no. 1 (January 1, 1905): 35–39; 48; "'The Wright Brothers' Flying Machine to Date," *Gleanings in Bee Culture* 33, no. 23 (December 1, 1905): 1,258.

Chapter 26

182. "New Medina Judge Needed; Expect Courthouse Problem," *Akron Beacon Journal*, July 30, 1965, 61; "Bill Approved; Await Signature of Gov. Rhodes," *Akron Beacon Journal*, July 30, 1965, 61; "Study New Layout for County Courts," *Akron Beacon Journal*, December 7, 1965, 74.

183. "Courthouse Addition Coming to Medina?," *Akron Beacon Journal*, February 1, 1966, 9; *Medina County Gazette*, February 7, 1966, 1; "Residents Are Complaining About Courthouse Addition," *Medina County Gazette*, February 7, 1966, 1, 2; "County Commissioners Are 'Open' to Suggestions About Courthouse," *Medina County Gazette*, February 10, 1966, 1; "Beauty or Beast? Medina Groups Debate Courthouse Addition," *Akron Beacon Journal*, February 17, 1966, 81; "Complaint Petition Filed On Courthouse Addition," *Medina County Gazette*, March 6, 1966, 1.

184. "Preview Slated on Courthouse," *Akron Beacon Journal*, June 14, 1966, 69; "Courthouse Plans Viewed by Public," *Akron Beacon Journal*, June 21, 1966, 53.

185. "Courthouse, Medina Income Tax Issues Are Voted Down," *Medina County Gazette*, November 9, 1966, 1, 2; "New Courthouse in Roman

Style," *Medina County Gazette*, September 14, 1968, 1; "Majority Favors Courthouse Plans," *Medina County Gazette*, June 23, 1966, 1; "Passage of 1-Mill Levy Would Solve Overcrowded Courthouse Facilities," *Medina County Gazette*, November 4, 1966, 15; "Courthouse Addition Plans Are Revealed," *Medina County Gazette*, June 21, 1966, 1, 2; "Mayor Gives Opinion on Architecture," *Medina County Gazette*, February 9, 1966, 1; "Courthouse Addition to Start Immediately," *Medina County Gazette*, December 15, 1966, 16; "Court Woes Plague Commissioners," *Medina County Gazette*, December 28, 1966, 1.

186. "Take a Look at Courthouse," *Akron Beacon Journal*, January 7, 1969, 101; "Dedication Plans Set for Courthouse," *Medina County Gazette*, December 10, 1968, 1.

187. "Dishonest Officials," *Lima Daily News*, May 4, 1895, 2; "Solicited Bribes," *Defiance Evening News*, June 28, 1895, 1; "Wood County: A Storm Center of Corruption," *Defiance Democrat*, February 28, 1895, 2; "Yost & Packard Exonerated," *Marion Star*, February 29, 1896, 1; "Solicited Bribes," *Defiance Evening News*, 1; Wood County Ohio Auditor, "Wood County Courthouse History," www.auditor.co.wood.oh.us.

Chapter 28

188. "Ribbon Cut on Renovated Vietnam Veterans Memorial," *Medina Gazette*, November 10, 2019, 1; Vietnam Veterans of America, "Chapter 385 Rededicates Memorial," www.vva.org; "Ground Breaking; Medina County Vietnam, Veterans Memorial—Gets a Facelift," *Medina County Veterans Newsletter* 11, no. 4 (Spring 2019): 4.

Chapter 29

189. "Our Opinion: Die Another Day?," *Akron Beacon Journal*, November 26, 2002, B2.

Chapter 30

190. Jefferey K. Taubenberger and David M. Morens, "1918 Influenza: The Mother of All Pandemics," *Emerging Infectious Disease* 12, no. 1 (January

2006): 15; "Flu Situation Better: Ban Partially Lifted," *Medina Sentinel,* January 3, 1919, 1; "Flu in County Still Prevails: Doctors Busy with Cases and Near Cases," *Medina Sentinel,* October 18, 1918, 1; "Epidemic Conditions Are Considered Over," *Medina Sentinel,* January 24, 1919, 1.

191. "Flu in County," *Medina Sentinel,* 1.

192. "Influenza Situation Remains About Same," *Medina Sentinel,* October 25, 1918, 1.

193. "Practical Joker Issues Warning to Every Voter," *Columbus Dispatch,* November 3, 1918, 3.

Chapter 31

194. Our World in Data, "Data from U.S. Public Health Service and US Center for Disease Control," www.ourworldindata.org; "Polio Epidemic Worst in History," *Cincinnati Enquirer,* December 22, 1952, 18; "Medina County Epidemic Far Exceeds the Worst Nation-Wide Polio Outbreak," *Medina County Gazette,* September 5, 1952, 1; "Medina Decides Against Polio Quarantine, Ban," *Akron Beacon Journal,* July 16, 1952, 28; "Polio Quarantine Proposal Balked," *News-Messenger* (Fremont, OH), July 16, 1952, 5; "Schools Will Have to Make Up Own Mind," *Medina County Gazette,* August 15, 1952, 1; "The Health Department and Poliomyelitis: Administrative factors in the 1952 outbreak in Wayne and Medina Counties, Ohio," *Public Health Reports, U.S. Public Health Service* 67, no. 11 (November 1952): 1,109–114; "Two-County Polio Virus Classified," *Medina County Gazette,* November 28, 1952, 1, 8; press releases, Medina Agricultural Society (June 3, 2020; June 11, 2020); press release of Ohio House of Representatives GOP Communications Department, June 9, 2020.

ADDITIONAL SOURCES

Chapter 5

American Yeoman (Brattleboro, VT). "Domestic Economy." April 8, 1817, 4.
Hartford Courant. "Domestic Economy." April 22, 1817, 2.
———. "Onandaga, July 10, 1816." July 23, 1816, 3.
———. "The Weather." October 15, 1816, 2.
William K. Klingaman and Nicholas P. Klingaman. *The Year Without Summer: 1816 and the Volcano That Darkened the World and Changed History*. New York: St. Martin's Press, 2014.

Chapter 11

Akron Beacon Journal. "Frank W. Woods Obituary." June 15, 1927, 24.
Akron Evening Times (Akron, OH). "Harding Leads 3 to 1: Wood Votes Lagging." April 28, 1920, 1.
———. "Republican Bosses to Get Opposition." February 28, 1920, 9.
———. "Woods Has Backers." April 21, 1920, 2.
Charles B. Galbreath. *History of Ohio*. Vol. 2. Chicago: American Historical Society Inc., 1925, 704–7, 711–13.
Cincinnati Enquirer. "Special Dispatch to the Enquirer by Herbert R. Mengert." June 19, 1927, 13.

Columbus Evening Dispatch. "Former State Solon Succumbs—Frank W. Woods." June 16, 1927, 22.

———. "New Taxing Board." January 21, 1909, 3.

Marysville Journal-Tribune. "Principle, Not Men Indorsed: Ohio Progressives Laud Both LaFollette and Roosevelt." January 2, 1912, 1.

Medina County Gazette. "Editor Comments." June 17, 1910, 4.

———. "Shall County Lines Decide It." June 17, 1910, 4.

Medina Sentinel. "County Chairmen to Sell War Bonds." December 14, 1917, 1.

———. "County Loan Quota Not Yet Reached." October 18, 1918, 1.

———. "Dogs of War Here on Saturday Night." September 27, 1918, 1.

———. "Governor Marmon and the Woods Bill." November 4, 1910, 4.

———. "Greatest Memorial Day Ever Held Here." June 1, 1917, 1.

Ohio House of Representatives, Membership Directory (1803–1966). Columbus, OH: Columbus Blank Book Company, 1966, 222.

Chapter 16

Butte Miner (Butte, MT). "Butte College of Music and Arts: Advertisement." May 28, 1916, 16.

Fremont Tribune (Fremont, NE). "Opens Music Studio Here." July 13, 1907, 6.

La Crosse Tribune (La Crosse, WI). "Professor CO Blakeslee in Recital at Presbyterian." November 3, 1928, 2.

Medina County Gazette. "Former Merchant Still Going Strong." February 12, 1954, 1.

———. "Many Cora Munson Blakeslee Secrets Will Remain—Secrets." April 13, 1979, 6.

———. "Medina County and Its People." September 28, 1956, 2.

Medina Sentinel. "Seville." September 6, 1907, 4.

Montana Standard (Butte, MT). "Brother of Butte Woman Dies." November 9, 1945, 9.

South Bend Tribune (South Bend, IN). "Condition is Serious." August 1, 1906, 5.

Spokane Chronicle (Spokane, WA). "Concert Company at Sunday Session." November 23, 1912, 17.

About the Author

Author Stephen D. Hambley, PhD, is a retired college professor and has been an elected official for roughly thirty years in various positions, including Brunswick City council member, county commissioner and state representative.